What Every Parent Wants for Their Child

and

How to Get It!

Jay Klusky, Ph.D.

U P T O N E
Press
Portland, Oregon

What Every Parent Wants For Their Child
and
How to Get It

by Jay Klusky, Ph.D.

Published by:
Uptone Press
4220 SE Aldercrest Rd.
Milwaukie, Oregon 97222

Klusky, Jay
What Every Parent Wants For Their Child
and How to Get It

ISBN: 0963401130
LCCN: 2009940249

$19.95 Paperback
Printed in the United States of America

Acknowledgements

It has been my profound good fortune to have had amazing teachers throughout my life. Dr. Barry Anderson at Portland State University guided me through my undergraduate years providing me with the encouragement and support I needed to make it to graduate school. Dr. Allen Parducci at UCLA was the best graduate advisor I could imagine. It was under Allen's wing that I began to grow as a scholar and learned to love writing. It was due to his lightness of being that my graduate years were three of the most fun and rewarding years of my life. These are my academic mentors.

Professor Leonard Trigg has been my martial arts teacher for the last five years. Only those in the circles in which he travels can understand what an astounding honor it is to be his student. Under his guidance I have become a much, much better teacher and because of my association with him my students have flourished more than they might otherwise have.

Which brings me to my dear friend, mentor, and colleague Dr. James Samuels. As of the writing of this book we have worked together for the past 35 years. As a young man he was both a father figure and mentor to me. As time passed our friendship grew, and as my education advanced we became colleagues. Much of what is written in these pages I learned under his tutelage. All the exercises outlined here are his. Please, make no mistake about it, I consider this book as much his as my own.

My deepest and humblest thanks to them all.

Also a special thanks to my brother Barry and colleague Peter who helped me edit this tome, (all the remaining errors are my own) and my good friend Dave who provided priceless help with the cover design.

Author's Notes

You will notice that there are Student Interludes after every chapter. These are two to four page essays written directly to teenagers. They are meant to be inspirational/motivational pieces for your son or daughter. They are also meant to be conversation starters; jumping off points from which you, your daughter, or your son can explore some of the ideas put forth in this book. Please use them as you see fit.

All the anecdotes in this book are recollections of actual events. I can vouch for recollections of episodes in which I was a part, though memory being what it is, I may have altered some of the minor details. As for those accounts that were related to me, I have endeavored to pass them on as accurately as my recall has allowed. Of course most of the names have been changed for obvious reasons.

One last note: As previously mentioned, I am deeply indebted to Dr. James Samuels for his contributions to this work. While he deserves credit for the exercises and many of the philosophical constructs, I am the one responsible for their interpretation. Therefore any mistakes or errors are mine and mine alone.

Enjoy the read!

Table of Contents

What Every Parent

Wants for Their Child

and

How to Get It!

Prologue

It was time for the talk. Isaac's father had been waiting for this day since his son was born. His father was a big bear of a man, both teddy and grizzly. His smile and his laugh could light up a room; he could also be tough as nails. Isaac loved him. It was the Sunday after Isaac's high school graduation and he cooked Isaac his favorite breakfast.

During the meal his father told him how proud he was of him; how proud his mother, grandmother and his sister were of him. He told him how all his aunts and uncles were thrilled that he made it through high school and did such a fine job. Isaac was moved by all the praise. It is special for a young man to be acknowledged by his father. But this was only one purpose of the talk. There was another.

"So what are your plans?" his father asked him easily.

"What do you mean, dad"?

"Now that you've graduated, what are you going to do?"

Isaac thought for a moment and said, "I was thinking about taken some time off, maybe travel, maybe get into my music . . ."

His father nodded and smiled as Isaac continued fantasizing about what he might do with his immediate future. Once Isaac finished his father leaned forward, put his hand on his son's knee, and said,

"As I see it you have two choices. You can either go to college, in which case our family will do what we can to help you, or you've got 60 days to find a job and get out of my house."

Four years later Isaac's dad was cooking his son's favorite breakfast. Isaac was the first member of the family to graduate college. Once again his father told him how proud the family was of him; what a great thing he had accomplished. Once again Isaac was moved. When they had finished eating his dad asked him to go wash his plate.

"Sure dad."

"Bring it here son." Isaac brought the plate to his father.

"Come with me." Isaac followed his father out onto the front porch of their house, at which point his father proceeded to take the plate and toss it as far as he could down the street. As the plate smashed into bits Isaac's father put his arm around his son's shoulder, turned to him, smiled with love and pride in his eyes and said,

"That was your last free meal."

Part 1

Laying the Groundwork

Parents can only give good advice or put them on the right paths, but the final forming of a person's character lies in their own hands.

Anne Frank

When I approach a child, he inspires in me two sentiments; tenderness for what he is, and respect for what he may become.

Louis Pasteur

Chapter One

What Every Parent Wants

The more people have studied different methods of bringing up children the more they have come to the conclusion that what good mothers and fathers instinctively feel like doing for their babies is best after all.

Benjamin Spock

So, what does every parent want for their child? Every parent wants their son or daughter to live a happy, healthy, and fulfilling life. If I could truly guarantee the health, happiness, and success of your daughter or son, most of you would happily give me almost anything you have. I would amass so much monetary wealth I'd make Bill Gates look like a pauper. Of course neither I nor anyone else can guarantee these things. I can, however, show you how to significantly increase the odds that the life your child leads will be amazing!

In the good old days, around the time most of you were born, many parents believed that if their children went to college and grew up to be good, kind adults everything would be fine. Some, to give their sons and daughters a leg up, endeavored to expose them to a wide variety of experiences . . . cultural, athletic, and natural. The more enlightened parents understood the important role good communication played in helping their children develop into the people they wished.

Some things don't change . . .

Having strong, truthful, open lines of communication between you and your children remains paramount. It is very important that your children can talk with you about anything and feel free to do so. Much of this book is dedicated to encouraging just that. Exposing your children to the arts, sport, and nature still helps them to be well-rounded and adds to the richness of their lives. Getting them excited about the activities you love, is one of the joys of parenting. Enlisting your family and friends to help with the pursuits that don't particularly interest you is an age old tradition. While these are a great beginning, today they are not enough.

The New Fundamentals

. . . and many do.

The world is changing rapidly. It is a very different place than it was even as recently as twenty years ago. The changes since the 1970's can make today's world almost unrecognizable. If you grew up in the 90's cell phone technology and the internet were in their infancy; you likely did not have access to them. Computers, by today's standards, were primitive and limited. There were no real laptops to speak of. If you did not have a set of encyclopedias at home you had to do research for school projects in a library. And if grew up in the 80's or earlier, well . . .

Yes, the world has changed; perhaps no more so than with regard to the futures available to your children. While there are many more career paths available to teenagers today, the paths are much less clear. Just a mere 30 years ago if you were raised in a factory town, there was a high probability you would get a job working in the factory. And that factory job paid well. It paid well enough for you to be solidly middle-class. It paid enough for you to buy a home, raise a family, take some vacations, and help your kids get through college. Not only did the job pay well enough, you could expect to have that job for life. If you were raised on a family farm, you likely would have ended up running the farm. Like the factory job, helping run the family farm also afforded you a stable middle-class life. If you were raised in a major city, life-long middle-class, white collar employment was also available.

Regardless of where you were raised, completing high school gave you a shot at the middle-class lifestyle. If you completed college, you were guaranteed to live better than that. Earning an advanced educational degree moved you even farther up the socio-economic ladder.

Today the paths are much less certain. Good paying manufacturing jobs are almost a thing of the past. Family farms are nearly history. A high school diploma will barely gain your daughter entry into the ranks of the working poor. The college degree that once was the guarantor of the good life now just gives your son a foot in the door. You can find people with master's degrees working as baristas at Starbucks. Fewer and fewer companies are providing life-long employment for their people.

Today, your children can expect to have three or four careers in their life . . . and these careers may be wholly unrelated. They may start out as an electrician and eight years down the road decide to go back to school and get into accounting. Fourteen years later they may go back to school again and become a teacher and twelve years after that they may find themselves owning a restaurant. Life can be that fluid.

Today, if your children are going to lead great lives they need to be highly adaptable and creative so they can position themselves to take advantage of opportunities as they arise. They need to be able to set their own course and have the self-discipline to persist until they succeed. Beyond networking they must be able to build meaningful relationships that they can sustain and that can sustain them throughout their lives. Most importantly, they need to be able to be optimistic and maintain their optimism in any and all circumstances.

These are the new fundamentals. These are the skills that will give your children the very best chance to have the lives you wish for them. These are the skill sets that will form the foundation from which they will have the very best opportunity to become extraordinary.

He's Not That Bright, He's Just Lucky

Every class has at least one. He never has to do much work and he always gets great grades. He aces every test and rarely has to study. He's super bright, a genius. Perhaps you're like him. Every class also has a few students who put in their time, work hard, and get A's.

Every class also has many, many more students who work hard to get the grades they get. Many of them struggle with one class or another. Sometimes they get A's, sometimes B's, often C's. Many of these students believe they're not bright, they're not cut out for school, and they're not like the smart kids. Some of them actually believe they're stupid. They couldn't be more wrong.

Students who get A's are more lucky than bright. Students who get A's easily are even luckier still. They are lucky to be born with a brain that processes information in a way that can take advantage of our school system. They are lucky that their body's chemistry allows them to sit and focus their attention on an adult in the front of a room for long periods of time. They are lucky that school interests them.

They are not unlike the boy who grows faster than his peers and so is the dominant athlete in junior high school. How many of you know a 12-year-old kid who just killed people on the basketball court or football field and never made his high school team? This was a kid destined for a professional career. He wasn't destined; he was just lucky he grew fast and had some coordination.

How many of you know exceptional high school athletes who were never heard of when they were in junior high school, kids who worked diligently and made the most of their abilities? Academics are no different.

In my 20 years of working with teens I have never, ever worked with a stupid one. I don't believe there's such a thing. Every teen I have worked with has been capable of being a B student, the majority have been capable of significantly more. All it requires is the willingness to do the work, the ability to keep going when you've made mistakes, and believing in yourself.

We are all born with gifts. Sometimes these gifts show themselves early, for instance musical ability, athletic ability, academic ability. Sometimes these gifts do not appear until later, for instance the ability to connect with people, the ability to make people laugh, the ability to see into the future. Sometimes these gifts do not readily appear at all and we have to go looking for them. Which ever category your gifts fall into, you have them. The game is finding them.

Being bright really has to do with how we develop and use our gifts. Being smart has to do with understanding our weaknesses and strengths, and knowing how to mitigate the former and take advantage of the latter. Being wise has to do with applying what we know so we can do the greatest good for the most people.

To paraphrase Napoleon Hill:

What you can conceive and believe, you can achieve!

Believe in yourself!!!

Chapter Two

Parenting in the 21ˢᵗ Century

Children have never been very good at listening to their elders, but they have never failed to imitate them.

James Baldwin

Enriching Your Child's Life

Parents are willing to go to great lengths to ensure their children's future. Parents play classical music to their babies in the womb in the hopes of improving their child's mathematical comprehension or perhaps developing a musical prodigy. When their children are just months old, parents enroll them in mother-baby classes. By the time they are two years old toddlers are in movement and music classes. At three they are learning to play an instrument and by the age of five they're engaged in organized sports. If the child shows any interest or aptitude for an instrument or a sport, by the time they are in high school their parents could have spent $25,000, $50,000, perhaps even more in the pursuit of their daughter's or son's activity. Often times they do so with the goal of college scholarships in mind. This is not to be sniffed at given the cost of higher education these days.

Does all this enrichment activity make a difference? Probably it does, to some degree. Do all these activities lead to prodigies? Probably not. Do they improve the odds of a child receiving scholarships to go to college? Maybe a little, though I suspect not as much as some parents hope. That being said, these efforts certainly can't hurt, unless, of course, parents take it too far . . . and sometimes they do.

We've all heard of parents going off the deep end with enrichment activities. You may have heard the story of Todd Marinovich back in the 1980's. From the time he was born his father began grooming him to be a professional football quarterback. I'm not kidding. Footballs were in his crib, his playpen, all over the house. His father began physically training him as an infant, stretching his son's hamstrings, having him on a balance beam before he could walk, and making sure he only ate the most nutritious foods. Todd was never fed anything with refined sugar or flour. He never had a fast food hamburger or an Oreo. As a toddler Todd was already being taught how to throw a football. Todd's entire life was focused on quarterbacking.

And this worked for a while. Todd set all manner of high school passing records and eventually was recruited by the University of Southern California. Todd was drafted into the NFL, did not live up to expectations, and eventually turned to alcohol and drugs. The last I heard he was in recovery and actually doing well. I believe, more often than not, this version of extreme parenting does not turn out as well as the parents intended.

Certainly, this is an unusual case. The vast majority of parents provide their kids with a number of opportunities and keep things in perspective. Providing your kids with as many of these types of enrichment opportunities is wonderful . . . yet they are only pieces of a larger puzzle. There are other activities that can have far greater impact on their futures. Some, outlined in this book will likely be new to many readers. Others, like the one that follows are as old as the written word.

Reading: Life-long Enrichment

Outside of a dog, a book is man's best friend. Inside of a dog it's too dark to read.

Groucho Marx

There is one academic enrichment activity that I believe is by far more important than all the rest combined: **READING TO YOUR CHILD.** If you have young children, please, please, please read to them every day. You can not start too early. Why is this so important? I am sure you all have noticed that children learn to speak pretty automatically. By the time children are about five years old they are speaking in full, grammatically correct, syntactically excellent sentences. They do so because their brains are hardwired to learn language between the ages of about 1 and 5 years old. Reading is part of this process. Consistently exposing your child to reading during these years will insure that they learn to read almost as readily as they learn to talk.

Learning how to read after this hardwired period becomes more difficult as time passes. It is very much like learning a second language. If your parents spoke a second language in the house when you were young, you likely learned it too. Even if you have forgotten it, picking it up again would be relatively easy. If, however, you first began learning a second language in middle school, your task is more difficult. Reading is very similar. By the time public schools begin to teach reading in the first grade when the students are about six years old, learning takes a lot more work.

Students who read well do much, much better in school than their peers who do not read with the same facility. So I implore you to please, please, please read to your children daily. One more thing, if you want to increase the likelihood of your children being good readers, you must also read. Children need to see that reading is a part of life; they need to see reading materials in the home and family members using them. Most often kids will do what their parents do. So, if reading is part of your life, it will become part of theirs.

Keeping it Real: The Apple Doesn't Fall far From the Tree

A few years ago a father called me seeking help with his son. His son was a junior and doing quite poorly academically. He had about 2.3 GPA. The young man was a good athlete; he was on his school's varsity baseball team. He was also good with electronics; he had a small, thriving business putting stereo systems in cars. He was a good kid, the neighbors all loved him.

So there I was sitting in the family's living room one winter evening. As the father explained the situation to me I could see he was upset. He believed it was so important for his son to do well in school. The young man's mother was quiet; she had heard of this before. The young man himself was reticent. After the father finished I turned my attention to his son.

"What do you think? Why aren't you doing well in school?"

He looked at me respectfully and said, "I'm not interested in school. I like working. I like my business."

I then turned to the father and asked, "How'd you do in school?"

"Oh I didn't do well at all. I hated it. I barely graduated with a C average. I did make it through a year of college though, and that's why it's so important for my son to do well in school."

"What did you do after your year of college?"

"I started my own retail appliance business."

I didn't have to ask the next question. He was obviously successful judging by the home I was sitting in.

"Well," I smiled. "It looks like your son is going to turn out just like you. He's going to struggle with school, but eventually get into business, be successful, and raise a strong family."

Mom nodded knowingly, "That's what I've been saying."

I can't begin to tell you how many conversations like this I have had. Parents who live very disorganized lives expect their daughter to be a paragon of order. Parents who never open up a book expect their son to enjoy reading. Parents who come home from work every night and have a few drinks call me when they find their daughter drinking with her friends. The apple rarely falls far from the tree. If you want to increase the chances of your children behaving a particular way, behaving that way yourself is a very good start.

We act out our values. If we truly value friendship, we will have good friends. If we really value learning, we will be educating ourselves. If we in fact value physical health, we will be taking care of our bodies. If we actually value love, we will express it often. Aware of it or not you will impart your true values to your children.

I am close with a couple who move through their lives at a frenetic pace. They almost religiously live beyond their means, and I'm not referring to their financial means. I'm referring to their energetic means. They are usually tired and often exhausted, their schedules are almost always overbooked, and most of what they do, they do in a tense way. Is it any surprise that their children also approach much of what they do with a lot of stress?

Stress and franticness are among the qualities this couple demonstrates they value. Did they plan to teach their children to engage with the world this way? Of course not. Take some time and observe your friends and their families. What qualities do they value? By your own actions, what qualities do you value? Are there other qualities you would prefer to pass on to your children?

What Teens are Thinking About

A few years ago I was running an after school program at a local junior high school. My students were seventh and eighth graders. One of them, Anthony, was one of the dominant males in the class. He was in eighth grade and big for his age. He was an exceptional athlete as well as a very good guitar player. He was sharp and he was good-looking. The girls loved him.

One afternoon he finished his assignment a little early and asked me if he could go out in the hall and practice his guitar. I gave him permission. Soon after another boy in the class, a young seventh grader, asked me if he could go out in the hall and practice his violin. That was fine with me. He was quickly followed by his friend, another young seventh grader, with his viola.

Now when I say young I mean somewhat immature, somewhat nerdy if you will. Both these young musicians were small of frame, not noticeably athletic, nor particularly attractive yet. About 20 minutes past and it was time to move on to the next subject, so I went out into the hall and called my three charges in. What I saw kept me laughing for days.

It seems that Anthony had taught the two young seventh graders a song and the three of them were jamming together. Surrounding the three young musicians were about 10 girls looking a bit like groupies. Anthony knew exactly what was going on. He was keenly aware of the gift he had given the two young seventh graders. Both of them floated into the classroom. The next day the violinist and the violist ran into class did their work amazingly fast, and asked me if they could go out in the hall and practice their instruments.

A few years earlier I was negotiating my fee to speak at a college in the state of Washington. The school's representative and I had been going back and forth a while when she offered me a deal. She suggested she'd be willing to give me my fee if, on the way to my talk, I would stop off at her son's junior high school and speak to his eighth-grade class about study skills. That was great with me.

The appointed day came and at ten o'clock, on a bright spring morning, I arrived at the junior high school. She was waiting there for me and brought me into the school's cafeteria.

"What are we doing in the cafeteria?" I asked

"You're speaking to my son's eighth-grade class," she replied.

"How many students are in your son's class?"

"Two hundred and twenty."

I panicked. Oh, I'm pretty sure it didn't show, but inside I was scrambling. I was expecting to speak to her son's class of about 30 students; it never dawned on me that I'd be speaking before the entire eighth-grade class. So there I was trying to figure out how I was going to get and hold their attention. I figured I had a minute, for if after a minute I didn't grab them, knowing what I know about kids that age, they would be gone . . . and I would be lost.

As the eighth-grade class began flooding into that cafeteria I was racking my brain when finally, just in the nick of time, I had an idea. The kids settled down, I took the mic, and asked,

"Who knows the most important reason to be educated?"

"So you can get a good job," one student responded.

"So you can understand the world," shouted another student.

"So you can make money," volunteered a third student.

"All good reasons," I said, "but they are not the most important reason." I paused for effect. "The most important reason to be educated is sex."

You could have heard a pin drop. I had their full attention. One teacher ran out of the room to get the principal.

I continued, "Okay girls, in about 10, 15, maybe 20 years most of you are going to be married or mated up in some way. How many of you want to be with a guy for 50 years who could only talk about football, and, on a good day, basketball?" A bunch of the girls laughed.

Now it was the boys turn. "Okay guys, in about 10, 15, maybe 20 years most of you are going to be married or mated up in some way. How many of you want to be with a gal for 50 years who could only talk about shopping and hair?" Now it was the guys turn to laugh.

Continuing, I got to the point. "The better educated you are the better chance you have of being a good patner and finding a good partner."

That was the last I said about sex. For the next 50 minutes I spoke about how to do well in school and get good grades. For those 50 minutes I had their undivided attention. I also learned a number of pretty valuable lessons. If I had any illusions that the vast majority of young teenagers were not thinking about sex, they were dispelled that day.

If you have a boy or girl who has begun to go through puberty, trust me, they are thinking about sex. Now they're probably not thinking about having sex yet, but they are beginning to think about those kinds of relationships and related subjects. Of course many kids are too embarrassed to talk with their parents about what's really going on, but you can bet they're thinking about it nonetheless.

Of course teens are thinking about other things besides sex. Many of them are thinking about how to remain kids. They're thinking about having fun with their friends. They're thinking about school, thinking about their family, thinking about jobs, thinking about politics, thinking about how to get what they want. They're thinking about life.

However, there is something they're thinking about that they almost never speak of . . . not even to themselves. This is the first generation in America that is unlikely to live as long as their parents. This is the first generation that is likely not to do as well financially as their parents. This is the first generation that is likely to have less stability than their parents. At a very deep level teens today have a sense of these realities and are troubled by them.

This is especially true in relatively affluent families, and by relatively affluent I am referring to upper-middle-class families. Kids from these families grow up very, very comfortably. They live in large homes. Their parents have lots of toys and they have access to them. Their parents provide them with many opportunities to recreate and vacation. They are aware at that deep level that once they leave their parent's home they will not live such a lifestyle. More importantly, many of them don't know how they will ever attain it.

Teenagers from considerably less affluent backgrounds in which education has not been stressed, have a difficult time seeing where the jobs will be for those without college educations. They do not see their way to fulfilling that old "American dream." It would serve all teenagers well for us to address these concerns with them, open up the discussion. As daunting as the future might seem to them, it is also rife with opportunity. It is our job to prepare them to identify and take advantage the opportunities that they will encounter.

The Fiction of Adolescence

Adolescence:

1. the transitional period between puberty and adulthood
    in human development, extending mainly over the teen
    years and terminating legally when the age of majority is
    reached; youth.

2. the process or state of growing to maturity.

    (Dictionary.com Unabridged Based on the

    Random House Dictionary, © Random House, Inc. 2009.)

We have come to assume many things about adolescence. We
assume adolescence is a time of rebellion. We assume adolescence
is a time of angst. We assume that during adolescence our kids
will lose their minds. We have come to assume adolescence takes
a long time.

We have come to accept adolescence as a given, but as recently
as 100 to 150 years ago it almost didn't even exist. As the Industrial Revolution got rolling, 14 and 15-year-olds were preparing to
enter the workforce, get married, and raise families. It wasn't until
early efforts to enforce child labor laws in the early 20th century
that the majority of teenagers began to have the luxury of time
to grow up.

It was only in the latter half of the 20th century that adolescence as a stage of development started to receive serious attention. As the result of this attention we consider all manner of
misbehavior and dysfunction to be "normal" adolescent behavior. I
cannot count the number of times I've seen teenagers grossly dis-
respect their parents only to have their parents shrug their shoulders, affect an embarrassed smile, and say something like, "Well,
he's a teenager."

Another result of this attention is the ever expanding time we
allow our youth to take before reaching maturity. When I was a
lad in the 1970's adolescence ended at about 18 when we were ex-

pected to either get a job or go to college. Last year "60 Minutes" did a piece in which psychologists were saying that we can now expect adolescence to last until our kids are about 30 years old.

They interviewed a college professor who told the story of a conversation in his office with one of his students. This particular student was not happy with her grade. In the midst of their discussion the student pulled out her cell phone, called her father, and gave the cell phone to the professor. Her father proceeded to try to get the professor to change his daughter's grade.

In the piece they also told of consultants who are being hired by Fortune 500 companies to instruct their managers in the special care and feeding of their 20 something-year-old employees. Once again the "60 Minutes" journalist interviewed one of these managers who told him of the time the mother of one of his employee's called him trying to get a raise for her son.

Is it any wonder some of our kids are taking until they are in their 30s to become functioning adults? Certainly it does not have to be this way. I have a dear friend who owns "Fierce Fitness Kickboxing," one of the best, if not the best, fitness center I have seen. He and his family run the business. One day while his wife was running class, he was in the office teaching his 12-year-old daughter Brittany, about the business.

During class his wife asked Brittany to come to the front of the class and demonstrate a particular exercise. She rushed to tie her shoes and ran out to help her mom. While she was helping out, he noticed that she didn't seem quite right; so after she was finished he called her back into the office and asked her what was wrong. After taking a moment to consider her father's question she said, "I wasn't professional." They proceeded to have a discussion about how she could be more professional, and when she went out to help her father with his class a few hours later, she was very happy with her performance.

A year later, Brittany was thinking about leaving public school. Her father asked me to help her and the family explore their options. Among the options I brought them was an elite private school with a considerable tuition. When I informed her dad of the cost of the school, he didn't bat an eye. He told me if his daughter wished to go she can just raise the money by marketing some programs at his fitness center.

I have had the pleasure of working with a number of students brought up with the expectation that they will be responsible for themselves from an early age. Brett was a senior at a local high school and one of the few students to ever call me wanting help with his study skills. (Almost always the parents make the call.) He was a soccer player with about of 2.7 GPA and, unlike most kids with a shaky GPA at this school, his parents were not noticeably concerned.

You see Brett was a little unusual. At the age of seven he started his own business mowing lawns. By the time he was twelve or so he expanded to doing other kinds of yard work, and by the time he was fifteen he had gotten into some light landscaping. As a junior Brett bought his first car and paid for the insurance with the money he earned from his business. He took his girlfriends out on his own dime, and even took responsibility for feeding himself. His parents weren't too concerned about his grades because they knew he would take care of business when it mattered . . . he'd been doing so since he was seven years old. The last I heard, Brett got into college with a scholarship to play soccer and was majoring in business.

The assumptions about adolescence are just that . . . assumptions. I have dozens of stories like Brett's. All over the world young men and women in their teens are doing pretty impressive things. I'm sure you know some. They may even be your own children. Our society underestimates the abilities and competencies of our youth and so puts fewer and fewer demands upon them. With so few demands, many of our youth have little opportunity to step up and show us what they can really do.

The Role of School in Today's World

The world has changed. Education is no longer the guarantor of the good life it once was. Today a bachelor's degree ensures little . . . a high school diploma, much less. High-paying manufacturing jobs are few and far between. Family farms are an endangered species. Simply getting a degree from a four-year institution will not gain your son or daughter entrance into the halls of affluent society. Actually, neither will a master's or doctoral degree. Mind you, all of the above will still increase their opportunities; education still remains an excellent first set of steps along the path to securing their future. It's just that education alone will not do it.

There was once a day when learning the 3R's: reading, 'riting, 'rithmetic was enough. Back in the 19th century public education was being established throughout our country with the primary goal of producing a workforce for the burgeoning industrial revolution. Joining this workforce in the 19th century required the equivalent of a fourth-grade education, so our educational system was developed with this in mind. Of course educational opportunities were available to those with greater interest and aptitude, but that was for a select few.

Back in those days all the education a person needed to become a functional member of the workforce was a fourth grade reading level, the ability to write a little bit, and some very basic math. In the early 20th century with the creation and enforcement of child labor laws, working parents needed some place safe for their children. Mandatory education through the age of sixteen became law and a high school diploma became the key that gained one entry into the workforce.

The bones of that system are still the structural underpinnings of our current public education system. Our system is trying to adapt, but like trying to turn an aircraft carrier around moving at full speed, adaptations occur very, very slowly. I suspect our society is evolving more rapidly than changes can be implemented. By the time some changes are implemented they are already behind the times. So what purpose does our educational system serve?

That's the type of question I probably get asked the most by my students. Their questions take the form,

"What is school for?"

"Why do I have to know _____?" (fill in the blank.)

"When will I ever use _____?"

These are all good questions and with the breaking of the guaranteed connection between education and income, having answers to these questions is critical for students to be motivated to do the work.

I believe that primary and secondary grade school serve two purposes. First . . . options. The greater success a student enjoys, the more options they have. Getting through school can no longer be simply about the diploma. Earning a high school diploma just is not enough. The real question is what options are available to you upon graduation? The same can be said for any college degree, undergraduate or advanced.

Not all people need to go to college nor should all people do so. But I will say that upon graduating from high school everyone should be ready to go to college. It is unwise for your son or daughter to finish high school believing that that is the end of their formal education. They do not know. How many of us are doing what we thought we would be doing when we left high school? My wish for my students is that they graduate high school prepared to go to college. In this way going to college or not is a true option, a true choice. And, if at some time in the future they believe college might be the way to go, they are not intimidated by the idea . . . they are ready.

Those who have taken care of their business academically have the confidence that those who did not take care of business generally lack. I have witnessed many people who were not successful in high school struggle as they confront going to college later in life. Many of them could have been successful if they would have paid attention to their studies when they were teenagers. Then going back to school would seem relatively easy.

What options are available and what opportunities can you take advantage of? These questions should play a significant role in your teen's thought process. How many directions can they go after high school? How many directions will they be able to go after college?

A second and equally important purpose for school is that school provides students a laboratory in which they can learn to become functional. School mimics the real universe . . . if we allow it to. During their time at school students will have goals to achieve, problems to solve, opportunities to explore, and mental toughness to develop. During their time at school students will have deadlines. During their time at school students will be asked to do things they do not want to do. During their time at school they will have events that challenge them.

If used properly school can help students become quite able people. In the real world, if one is to be successful, goals must be set, problems solved, deadlines met. If kids are to become successful adults they must develop the mental toughness to do things that they do not like, yet are critical for their success. Our kids can use school to develop the confidence to meet challenges head-on, knowing that they can make things work out well; and they will have many opportunities to do so.

Levels of Learning (Samuels)

A man only learns in two ways, one by reading, and the other by association with smarter people.

Will Rogers

While the 3R's are still a good idea, if that's all our children have they will be woefully unprepared to function in today's world. Even a good understanding of algebra, biology, history, and Shakespeare, though laudable to have, will not prepare them for the challenges and opportunities of the 21st century. They need to develop a new set of fundamental skills that will serve them in the highly fluid environment in which they will be living, working, and playing.

Skills, by definition, are things we learn, and in the learning of any skill we pass through stages. It is useful to be able to identify the stage one is in so you can see the path and know what to expect. Let's take a look.

In the learning of any skill, if we are to be successful, we will pass through three levels of learning: clarity, capability, and confidence. We will do so in that order. There are no shortcuts, circumventions, or other paths. It is only by successfully navigating each successive stage that we will pass go and collect two hundred dollars.

Clarity

The first stage is clarity. In order to learn a skill you have to first understand what it is you're working to learn. You have to be clear about it. How you gain clarity is an individual process. Some people gain clarity through understanding the logic of what it is they're learning. Other people gain clarity through seeing themselves applying the skill in their mind's eye. Still others gain clarity through feeling their body perform the skill. Most of us use some combination. However you get there, the greater clarity you have, the better you will perform.

When I was around 20 years old a dear friend, who was a kind of father figure to me at that stage of my life, taught me how to drive. I learned in a car with a manual transmission. Before he allowed me to even turn the ignition he spent a fair amount of time teaching me how the transmission worked and the roles the clutch, stick shift, and gas had in making the transmission engage the engine. This really helped me to see and feel what I was doing.

This is the stage many of us like to get through fast. We just want to move on and get to it. This is all well and good, but if we get to it without really understanding what it is we're getting to, our ability to do what we are learning will be diminished. If we take our time and pay close attention, transitioning to the next stage will happen naturally and easily.

Capability

Becoming capable requires practice . . . and not just any practice, the right practice. We've all heard the old saw 'practice makes perfect.' Actually, this is not completely accurate. More accurately, 'perfect practice makes perfect.' It is critical that we practice the right thing in the right way. We become capable when we, in fact, perform the skill correctly. It is here where the rubber meets the road. Can we do the skill repeatedly and consistently get it right. This is the mark of capability.

Once again, they are no shortcuts. Some people need one repetition to get it, others may need one thousand. If you're going to be capable you simply have to do the work, and if you're willing to do the work, there is little you cannot achieve. If your daughter or son is willing to do the work there is almost nothing s/he cannot accomplish.

If you learned how to drive a car with a stick shift, I'm sure you remember stalling the car out a number of times. Then you got it right. You put the car in first gear, stepped on the gas gently, lifted up the clutch, and the car moved forward smoothly. If you're like me you felt a sense of pride and accomplishment. Success! We can drive!

Not so fast. Because then, if you're like me, the next few times you stalled the car out again. Then we got it right a few times, then we stalled a few times, then we started getting it right a lot more than we stalled. Finally, we got it right almost all the time, as long as we focused. Then and only then were we capable!

We were able to do it well as long as we paid attention. This is the mark of the low end of capability. Over time, with the right practice, we got to the point where putting a car into first gear hardly required any attention at all. Not needing to pay attention in order to get it right indicates one has arrived at the top end of capability and is hitting the lower end of the next level of learning.

One last thought about capability. The level of capability one achieves is up to the individual. There are jump shots and then there are NBA jump shots. There's driving and then there is NASCAR driving. There's playing piano and then there's playing piano at Carnegie Hall. It is solely up to each person to decide how capable they will work to become. The sky is truly the limit.

Confidence

Confidence is the final level of learning. When you are certain you can perform a skill as well as you would like you have achieved confidence. As with capability, the path to confidence is correct practice. Confidence is not to be confused with bravado or empty assertions of ability. It cannot be faked, it can only be earned. One does not achieve confidence by simply reciting self-affirmations. To achieve confidence one has to gain the clarity and put in the practice required to become certain of their capability.

Of course these levels are not discrete; one does not become perfectly clear and then work at becoming capable. What actually happens is that one becomes clear enough to practice and as they practice their capability rises. At the same time, their practice helps them become even clearer, which in turn allows them to become more capable. As they become more and more capable their confidence grows, and as their confidence grows their trust in their capability also grows to the point where they are fully confident.

.

Student Interlude

Getting What You Want
From Your Parents

Your parents are very simple creatures. If you could step inside their heads you would see that a large proportion of their thoughts and feelings center around you. If you looked a little closer you would notice that their thoughts and feelings are of two general types: fear/worry and excitement/pride. Of these, your parents probably spend a whole lot more time worrying about you and your future. It's not their fault, parents are wired this way. If you have children you will understand. For now, trust me.

Your parents want one thing far and above all else. They want it so much, that if I, or anyone else, could provide it, they would give us almost everything they own. What is it they want? Simple. They want a guarantee that you will be healthy, happy, and fulfilled. Now, they know they cannot have that guarantee and this is what they worry about. They worry that you won't be healthy. They worry that you won't be happy. They worry that you will go sideways and your life will not be fulfilling.

Since there are no guarantees, each and every day your parents look for signs that you are heading in the right direction. Were you kind to your sister? Did you do your homework? Did you help your grandmother around her house? Did you practice your piano? Did you do your chores? Did

36

you volunteer at the animal shelter? These are all indicators to your parents that you are heading down the right road.

But doing all these things doesn't guarantee your future? Of course not. Do all straight A students live great lives? Don't be silly. But that's not the point. The point is that markers, like your grades, point in a particular direction in the minds of your parents.

So, I ask you, what would you like to get from your parents? Would you like something material, perhaps an iPod, or a cell phone, perhaps access to a car? Would you like more freedom? Maybe you would simply like your parents off your back.

The magic to getting any and all of these and more is based on this understanding of your parents. If you do those things that show your parents you are on the right track as they see it, they will only be too happy to give you what you want. That's all there is to it. For the most part all you have to do is be a good person and take care of business in school. If you do these you will allay many of their fears and they will make your life easier and easier.

Chapter Three

The Fine Art of Motivation

All men dream: but not equally. Those who dream by night in the dusty recesses of their minds wake in the day to find that it was vanity: but the dreamers of the day are dangerous men, for they may act their dream with open eyes, to make it possible.

T. E. Lawrence

I have never worked with a dumb student. I have yet to meet the student who could not excel in middle school or high school. I have, however, met many students who were not motivated to do so. To be sure school comes easier to some students than others. We all knew students who never seemed to do much work and always got high grades. We believed they were the bright ones. Some of us even called the most outstanding of those 'bright' students geniuses.

Our children are no different. If school does not come easy to them, all too often they believe they're not the exceptional ones. This is very unfortunate because these kinds of assessments usually result in diminished motivation. It is even more unfortunate because such assessments are not true. Many of the so-called 'bright' students are more lucky than bright. They are lucky that their learning styles fit the school system of today. They are lucky that they have a natural ability to remember little bits of information. Intelligence, brightness, being smart, have much more to do with what your children make of their gifts than the gifts themselves.

To repeat: I have never worked with an incapable student. I have mostly worked with students who either have yet to develop the tools they need to succeed or lack the motivation to excel. Providing a motivated student with the tools for success is fairly easy and straightforward. (Check out my first book, *"Easy A's Winning the School Game."*) Helping a student develop the motivation to do the work is an art form, one at which I continue to strive to master.

Starting Where They Are

The year was 1992. I was running a family literacy program that met in a church every Saturday morning. Every week about fifteen parents and their children showed up to work on the kids' reading and writing skills. The students ranged in age from six to fourteen. One Saturday morning Pam, the mother of Willis, came to speak to me privately during one of our breaks. She told me that her son, who was in eighth grade, just failed his last science test. She went on to tell me that this was particularly troubling because Willis wanted to be a doctor.

By this time I had known Willis about four or five months. I knew of his aspirations, and found him to be quite gifted. In fact, science and math were his strengths. He was also an avid reader, a leader in our class., so much so that he was being paid a small stipend to assist with the younger students in the program. Willis was one of the few kids in his peer group who watched "Nova" religiously.

He was also involved in a medical mentor program. During the first day of the program the medical students took all their charges down to the morgue at the hospital. I suspect it was their way of having fun; almost nobody holds their food down the first time. Not only did Willis easily hold his food down, he was so excited he actually put his hands in one of the bodies and tried to identify as many organs as he could. He was no ordinary eighth grader. I liked him very much and you can bet I was not happy to hear about his science exam.

When class resumed I announced to the class,

"We have to have a talk with Willis here. It seems he wants to be a doctor yet failed his science test. Willis, what's up with that?"

Before Willis could get a word out his mom looked at him sternly and said,

"Tell him the truth. Don't tell him what you told me, tell them the truth."

Both Pam and I were trying to get Willis to take responsibility for that test, but Willis wasn't quite ready to do so. Instead he gave me the old, tired party line,

"Ms. Richards hates me. She's always hated me. She hates all of us. She's the worst teacher in the school. She doesn't care about us and she can't teach."

Pam was glaring at him, when to the astonishment of us both, another student in the class shouted out, echoing Willis's assessment. This was followed by that young girl's mother backing her daughter up. Perhaps Ms. Richards really was as bad as Willis suggested.

I stood up, walked over to Willis, and looked at him empathetically.

"Do you think she really hates you?" He nodded affirmatively.

"You don't like her either, do you?" He nodded again.

"Do you want to get even with her?" He sat up straight and I could see the fire begin to glow in his eyes as he nodded one final time.

"Get A's. If she really does hate you, it will piss her off."

Three weeks later Willis had another science test. He showed up to our program and proudly told us he received the highest mark in Ms. Richards' three classes. Pam told me all she had to do was remind Willis of my suggestion the night before the test. He took it from there. The fact that he did so well did not surprise me in the least; I knew what he was capable of. What was surprising however was the girl who backed him up that morning three weeks ago, a girl that had demonstrated little interest in science or math, received the third highest grade.

To be sure, 'getting even' is not the most high-minded, altruistic of motivations. It was, however, the motivation that Willis responded to in that time and place. You have to start where people are for your best chance of success. It is why connecting educational achievement to sex grabbed the attention of the eighth-graders at that middle school in Washington. If you're going to effectively motivate your children it will be to your great advantage to understand where they are truly coming from; not where you would like them to come from; where they are actually coming from.

We all know that doing well in high school increases one's chances of getting into a good college and that getting into a good college increases one's chances of having greater opportunities upon graduation. This is logical and makes perfect sense to us. To some ninth graders this makes no sense at all. To many other ninth graders this may make sense one day, when they're reasonable, and sounds like gibberish the next. You know, like when they're "in love."

To a large degree, when we're talking about teenagers, it's more important **that** they take care of business than **why** they take care of business. After all, is there any real difference between a 16-year-old guy who diligently practices piano in order to attract girls and a 16-year-old guy who diligently practices piano as an outlet for self expression? And we can certainly hope that the quality of their motivations will improve with their level of maturity.

Inside or Out? Motivation's Age Old Question

Some of the questions I most frequently get asked have to do with the best methods of motivating kids. The majority of these questions boil down to the issue of internal versus external motivations. Many parents are concerned with the perceived deleterious effects of externally motivating their children to do well in school. After all, isn't it best that our children learn to do the work for its own rewards? Isn't it best that our children find their own drive to succeed?

Yes. I believe it certainly would be best if our children were motivated by their own internal desires; though how many of you would continue working at your jobs if your salary was cut by 75%? You see, it is human nature to be motivated by both internal and external forces. A few years ago I had the pleasure of sitting in on my mentor and colleague Dr. Jim Samuels' class when one of his students complained about her job being boring.

"They're paying you for it, aren't they?" he began. "If this activity you're complaining about was really meant to be fun you'd be paying them. That's what we call entertainment. The fact that you don't find the work you're doing fun is why they're paying you for it. They would likely have a hard time finding someone to do that work for free. Of course, if you'd rather do different work, do what you need to do to put yourself in position to do that different work. Optimally, you will set yourself up so most of the work you do you will find enjoyable. Better still, you can learn how to bring enjoyment to all you do. Until then, enjoy that you're getting paid."

Among some purists external rewards get a bad rap. Is there really much of a difference between working for inner satisfaction and working for grades or something your grades may buy you? The line can be very gray. In the end we're working for feelings: the feeling of satisfaction or the feeling the reward brings us. Besides, just like us, kids will do the work when the work actually interests them. If they are not interested in global studies, putting in a little something to sweeten the pot isn't necessarily such a bad idea.

So, my answer to the question of internal and external rewards is: use whatever works. Actually it's not as much a question of internal or external, it's more a question of what buttons need to be pushed to get the job done. Sometimes it takes strong validation, sometimes an iPhone. Sometimes it takes going to a ballgame, sometimes more freedom. Sometimes it takes access to a car, sometimes love.

Then again, sometimes it takes cold cash. A few years ago I was called in to help with a high school sophomore. He was your typical bright kid who wasn't doing much school work. He, his father, mother and I were sitting around the dining room table (it seems like so much of my work takes place in dining rooms) and discussing the situation. The father, trying to understand what was going on asked his son why he wasn't doing his work.

"It's boring. I'm not interested. Come on it's not like it's a job!" the boy answered. Little did the young man know the mistake he had just made . . . he was about to find out.

His father leaned back in his chair thoughtfully and his mien began to change. Then he came forward with a different set of his spine, looked at his son with steely eyes and said,

"Now it is. From now on, aside from food, you get nothing from us. You have enough clothes to last you a couple of years. You have your room and you live in this house. That's it. If you want an allowance, you'll have to bring home grades. If you want to go snowboarding with your buddies, you'll have to be doing your homework. If you want anything from us other than the basics, you'll have to be taking care of your business." He was on a roll. "Of course if you'd rather continue not doing your work, that's fine with us too. On Friday and Saturday nights you can bring your girlfriend home and we can all watch movies together."

The family proceeded to set up a fee schedule: small assignments were worth so much, large assignments were worth more, tests were worth X amount of dollars, grades at the end of each grading period were worth Y amount of dollars. The young man's grades substantially improved.

I'm not going to say this is the best approach. I am also not going to be critical of it. It worked . . . and whatever works, within the bounds of the law and decency, is fine with me. Over the course of my work I have seen many, many different approaches get good results. I will say positive reinforcements are preferable to negative reinforcements. Where there's a choice it is better to give children rewards, material or otherwise, in return for good work rather than punishments for lack thereof. As parents, the guiding principle should be doing whatever works, so long as you deem it comfortable for yourself and appropriate for your family.

The Long and Short of It

While we're on the subject of rewards and punishments it is important to consider the long and short term. Whether we are addressing work in school, chores at home, or encouraging your son to grow into a caring person, the timing of your reinforcement is important.

As early as middle school, and at times even earlier, parents are setting up reward structures for good grades. Typically, kids can get some significant reward if they bring home a certain GPA.

This is all well and good; however, it does not take advantage of all the motivational powers rewards can generate. A reward for attaining a certain GPA is just one kind of temporal reward, a long-term reward. Rewards for long-term accomplishments get their power from the significance of the reward to the student. I've seen parents promise European vacations, cars, permission to play sports, ski lift tickets, all manner of electronic gear, and more in return for a good grade report. So what happens when halfway into the semester it becomes apparent to the student that the goal of a 3.75 GPA is very unlikely? Their motivation can go down the tubes.

A good idea is to mix in rewards for short-term accomplishments as well. These kinds of rewards get their power from the increased likelihood of success. Though they may not be as significant, nor should they be, as rewards for long-term accomplishments, they can go a long way towards keeping your daughter or son motivated through to the accomplishment of the longer-term goal.

Rewards such as making your daughter's favorite meal, having some of your son's friends sleep over, going out to their favorite restaurant, going to their favorite park, allowing them more computer gaming time, are just some of the short-term type of rewards parents have found effective.

Whether we're talking about long or short term rewards, it is important to ensure that the reward is actually something your child wants. I know this may sound quite obvious; however, it is not unusual for parents to put out rewards that really do not motivate their children. So I just point this out here as a caveat. Stay close with them and understand what is truly important to them. I've seen parents get a good year's work out of their daughter simply in return for letting her get her ears pierced.

Here's another that falls in the obvious category and I want to mention it just for clarity's sake. In the best of worlds the short-term accomplishments you require in order for your child to be rewarded should build upon each other and lead to the long-term accomplishments you both seek. Pretty obvious,. You might be surprised at the number of families that have long-term rewards based on academic accomplishments and short-term rewards based on doing chores at home. Please understand that you're free to set up as many reward structures as you like. If both academic achievement and neatness at home are important, set up two groups of short and long-term rewards.

The Failure, Determined, Careless Cycle

This is a pattern you might be familiar with. It is a pattern all too common among teenagers, as well has many of us adults. I have some bad and some good news regarding this pattern. The bad news is that when we are bound into this pattern success is highly unlikely. The good news is that breaking the pattern is fairly straightforward. If you're going to really help your children you need to be aware of it, know how to identify it, and know how to short circuit it so they can move beyond this pattern and succeed.

So how does the failure/determined/careless cycle work? It's actually pretty simple. It works like this: your daughter isn't doing well at school and you are unhappy. This is the failure phase. As a result you get on your daughter's case, you punish her to show your dissatisfaction and to 'encourage" her to get her act together. Perhaps you ground her or take away her cell phone.

Your daughter, wanting her privileges restored and you off her back, bears down and gets to work. She makes up all her homework, studies for all her tests, and makes sure her grades are where you need them to be. This is the determined phase. Your daughter becomes determined to improve. As a result of her newfound enthusiasm for her work her grades go up. Her teachers tell you she has all her homework in; she has received high marks on her recent tests, she even looks happier. All is right with the world. You are happy with her progress and restore her privileges.

So far so good. Things are going so well for her, her grades have improved so much, that when one of her teachers assigns the class a small 10 point project she decides she can blow it off. After all things are going well and it's a really not worth much. Two days later she forgets another assignment. Then she has some homework to do, plans to get it done over the weekend, but is too busy hanging out with her friends. This is the careless phase of the cycle.

After a while she gets increasingly careless and her grades begin to suffer. You find out, get angry, and the cycle begins again. So goes the failure/determined/careless cycle. People get bound by this all the time. Things aren't going well, we focus our attention until things are going better, then we take our attention off and things degenerate.

So how do we free ourselves? While not necessarily easy, the answer is simple. Focus longer. Focus until the goal is accomplished. This implies that you have a clear goal that will do the job. So, instead of demanding that your daughter's grades improve, which is somewhat vague, (going from a D- to a D is, after all ,an improvement), decide with your daughter what is an acceptable level of improvement. You may decide that a reasonable goal is to have all her homework complete and up to date by Friday of every week, and earn B's or better on each of her tests. In many schools teachers make all this information easily accessible to parents online. In most schools teachers are happy to send a report home at the end of each week telling parents whether or not their son or daughter is current on their work. Such a goal will help her keep focused long enough for her to succeed. Whatever you choose, the key is to stay on it until the goal is accomplished.

Helping Kids Find Their Own Motivation

> *Some of the world's greatest feats were accomplished by people not smart enough to know they were impossible.*

Doug Larson

We've discussed motivating kids externally; now let's look at helping them develop their own motivations. The key to helping your children find their own motivations is being free to support their dreams. I have never told one of my charges they cannot do something. Only in the case of harmful or illegal activities have I ever told a student of mine they should not do something. I have always encouraged my students to pursue any path they wish, provided it was legal and healthy.

I have worked with dozens of students who have wanted to be fashion designers, more who have wanted to be musicians, and probably hundreds who wanted to be professional athletes. I've worked with students who wanted to be actors, fighter pilots, writers, engineers, doctors, lawyers, film directors, the list goes on. I have even worked with one student who wanted to be a roller coaster designer. I have sat in the homes of a number of these students and watch their fathers, mothers, sisters, brothers, and older relatives try to discourage them. I've seen counselors and teachers try to dampen their enthusiasm. I've seen their 'friends' try to dissuade them.

In most cases, all these people mean well. Certainly they are all being reasonable. After all, what are the odds of having a career as an actor or film director? Do you know how few people get to be jet pilots? Or a rock star? Give me a break!

When a young man who is 5'8", can't jump, and doesn't shoot worth a darn, tells me his goal is to make it into the league, I tell him that that's a great goal. Then I tell him what he needs to do to accomplish it. You see, I have worked with athletes who've played

Division I college basketball, and I have even worked with a couple that made it to the league.

I tell him about my friend's son who's not much taller than he is who played point guard for the University of Oklahoma. I tell him all the hours my friend's son put into developing his game. Then I tell him about the young man I know who started for the University of Kansas for four years and how he got the opportunity to play in part because he was good, and in larger part because he was a 4.0 student. I tell him how important it is to not only work on his game, but work on his grades. I do whatever I can to connect his dream with the work I know he needs to do in order to be successful if his particular dream is not realized.

Time and time again, parents, teachers, and counselors failed to take advantage of the awesome motivational power of a young person's dreams. You want to be an actor? You'll need to develop strong public speaking skills and stage presence. You'll also want to go to the best acting school you can. This means making sure your grades are exceptional. Get to work!

You wanna be a rock star? Let me tell you about my friend who's drummed for Billy Idol, Foreigner, Cher, and is currently working with Pink. Let me tell you how many years it took him, how many doors he pounded on, how many demos he delivered to get to where he was considered for these gigs. Of greater import, let me tell you about all the work he did to make himself into the great, supportive, uptone man he is today; the man all these artists love to work with. You can do this too. You'll need to develop an almost inhuman ability to persist. Of course surrounding yourself with some of the best young artists can increase your chances of fulfilling your dream, and do you know where the best young artists hangout? Many of them hang out at the best music conservatories and if you want to get into those conservatories not only do you have to work your ax, you have to have the grades to get in. Get to work!

If I don't know the fundamentals of making it in a particular field, I will have the student do some research. I have learned that I do not have the ability to predict with certainty who will be successful. I believe it is our job as parents, counselors, teachers, and mentors to provide those we are responsible for with the best, most accurate, most inspiring information possible.

This brings us back to freedom. If we are going to do all we can to help those we care for find their own motivation, we must be free for them to pursue any path, even if that path looks like a dead end to us. Equally as important, we must be free to let them fail or succeed. It is then incumbent upon us to help them pursue that path in a way that ensures they will be more ready and more able to pursue their next path.

To Medicate or Not to Medicate:
A Different Kind of Test for ADHD

There has been much controversy over the diagnosis of Attention Deficit Hyperactivity Disorder (ADHD) in our society in recent years. Some doctors, psychologists, and counselors believe it is a disorder affecting a significant number of our kids. It would be considered epidemic in its scale if it were contagious. Certainly it is not. Other doctors, psychologists, and counselors believe ADHD is largely over-diagnosed and simply speaks to behaviors that are normally exhibited by young boys. In the spirit of full disclosure I tend to lean towards the latter. I will say that when I hear a girl has been diagnosed with ADHD my ears perk up because of the rarity of the occurrence. This being said, this is neither the time nor the place to review all the literature on all sides of this controversy. I leave it up to the reader to research ADHD to their satisfaction.

Many parents wrestle with the decision to medicate or not medicate their children when there is an apparent diagnosis of

ADHD. I truly feel for these parents. Personally, I have taken precious little medication in my life and have an underlying belief that the less, the better. However, I have seen children of my friends experience benefit from medication for ADHD.

I would like to propose a test you can do at home to perhaps help you make a more informed decision. We notice that many children with this diagnosis seem unable to focus on their schoolwork yet can engage intently with a computer game or some other activity they are highly interested in for long periods of time. Doctors suggest that this ability to hyper-focus is part of the condition. Others suggest that this is an indication of a motivational component to the behavior.

Here's a test I recommend. Find out something your son really, really, really wants . . . within reason. If, for instance, you have noticed he has difficulty attending to his math homework, offer to give him what he wants if he completes his math homework within an agreed upon amount of time. Of course he has to get most of the homework correct. Do this test two or three times over the course of a month or so. If he can do the homework well in the agreed upon time, it is more likely your son's attention issues are issues of motivation rather than issues of attention.

I have seen estimates of ADHD incidence ranging from a low of 3% to a high of 10% with boys 2 to 3 times more likely to be effected.* This would suggest that at the high end of this range two or three students in any given class might be on medication. I have been in a number of classes in which two, three, and even four times that number were being medicated. Something does not quite add up. I suspect that a number of students will attend to their work with much greater focus when adequately motivated.

* www. childtrendsdatabank.org/indicators/76ADHD.cfm

20 Years or 3

How many of you are planning to go to college? I suspect that a lot of you are. Good. How many of you know what college really costs? I suspect only a few. You really need to know so you can make the best choices you can during your high school years. All throughout high school we are faced with ostensibly the same choice each and every day. Do we take care of our academic business or do we do something else?

It's Saturday morning, you have a major project due on Wednesday and your friends are going skateboarding. What do you do? A lot of you will go skateboarding: after all, you could always work on Sunday and you still have Monday and Tuesday. On Sunday another friend calls you up with an extra ticket to the NFL game. Now these don't come along often so rather than work you go to the football game. You're able to get a little work done on Sunday night and a little more Monday but you still have a lot to do, so Tuesday night it is. Tuesday afternoon, just as school ends, you find out one of your close friends got into a serious fight with his parents, left home, and needs a place to stay. This is a real emergency and you are a good friend so you convince your parents to let him stay with you for a few nights. You spend Tuesday evening helping him. You never do get your assignment done.

Sound familiar? You certainly made the right choice on Tuesday, and you might have even made the right choice on Sunday, but I would say you blew it on Saturday. Why? Because you say you want to go to college . . . and college is expensive . . . and you, by simply choosing to go skateboarding, significantly diminished your chance to get your college paid for.

Do you take care of your academics or do you do something else? Really taking care of your academic business requires you to be focused on doing your work, and doing your work before you go and play . . . for about three years. Now, when you're 14 or 15 years old three years can seem like a long time, but as long as it may seem it's nowhere near as long as 20 years.

Let's run some numbers and I think you'll see what I mean. Tuition, room and board, fees and books at the average state college or university costs between $15,000 and $20,000 a year. Multiply that by four years and the average college education at a state school is going to cost anywhere between $60,000 and $80,000. A four year education at a private college or university in 2009 will cost between $200,000 and $250,000. All these costs will likely increase over the next few years.

Let's say you focus on your studies and work your rear end off in high school. You will likely put yourself in a strong position to have one or more colleges offer you scholarships. You will also put yourself in a strong position to receive grants from sources other than colleges. If you do well enough you can get your entire college education paid for. If you do, you will graduate college without owing any money to anyone.

Let's say you don't focus on your studies as well as you know you can and you don't do all that much work during high school. You will likely not be in a strong position to receive scholarships or grants. If your parents can help pay for college, I'm sure they will. How-

ever, few families have the means to foot an $80,000 bill, especially if they have a number of children. So you are going to have to take out loans.

If you have to take out loans for your entire education at a state school you will graduate owing approximately $70,000. If your loans came with a 7.5% interest rate and you were to pay it off in 20 years, you would have to pay $540 a month for 240 months. If you do the math your education will not have cost you $70,000, it will have cost you $129,600. Almost double.

Let's say between your family and our government you could come up with half the cost of your education so you only have to borrow $35,000. You would still be paying about $280 a month for 240 months for a grand total of $67,200. By the way, we have not taken into account the cost for furthering your education beyond college. Perhaps you want to go to medical school, perhaps get a Masters of Business Administration, or perhaps get your Ph.D. They all cost money, and like college, if you perform at a high level you can get them all paid for.

You're going to pay for your education one way or another. You can pay for it now while life is pretty easy, your food, clothing, shelter, and much of your entertainment is being paid for by your family, simply by taking care of your academic business. Or, you can pay for it in cash later, when you have to pay for your own existence. Like almost everything else in your life, what you do is up to you.

So, next weekend when you have work to do and your friend calls to go and hang out . . .

Chapter Four

Growing a Brain:

Connecting Actions to Consequences

The person who in view of gain thinks of righteousness; who in the view of danger is prepared to give up their life; and who does not forget an old agreement however far back it extends — such a person may be reckoned a complete person.

Confucius

I first heard the expression 'growing a brain' from Dr. Joy De-Gruy, a doctor of social work research. She used it to refer to what kids need to do before they were ready to be on their own. Growing a brain has to do with one's ability to see into the future, consider the consequences of one's actions, and make intelligent choices.

Five-year-olds have very little of their brains grown; they usually can't see much past today. Telling a five-year-old on a Tuesday that 'if they cooperate we can go to the zoo on Saturday' rarely computes. They'll hear 'the zoo,' but Saturday probably won't make much sense. Ten-year-olds have more of their brains grown; they can consider days, even weeks in advance; fifteen-year-olds even more so.

While, most young teenagers believe their brains to be fully grown, we know better. Many have not quite yet connected the dots. They often cannot quite yet see past their urges to the consequences of acting upon their urges three, five, and ten years into their future. Usually, sometime around their junior or senior year, their brains have a major growth spurt (I mean this figuratively, of course) as the reality of life after high school dawns on them.

What's a Parent to Do?

Parents have many responsibilities. There are the bare-boned legal responsibilities: making sure your children have adequate food, clothing, and shelter; making sure they are safe, and making sure they have good medical care. Then there are the 'extra' responsibilities all good parents assume: to do your best to ensure they have adequate stimulation when they are young; ensure they're well educated; provide them the best opportunities for growth that you can; and above all, love them.

Parents also take it upon themselves to secure their children's future to the best of their abilities. How you go about meeting these responsibilities goes a long way toward determining how prepared your children are for the futures that awaits them. Parents want their children to have better lives than they had, they wish to shelter their children from many of the hardships they have experienced. Parents want their children's lives to be easier than their own.

In an effort to fulfill these wishes many parents find themselves confronted with a deep dilemma: what happens if by doing all you can for your children you make them less able? When does providing a better life diminish self-initiative? These are particularly relevant questions for parents of even modest means; even more so for parents who have achieved some level of financial affluence. Because as parents work to make their children's lives easier they often inhibit the 'growth of their children's brains.'

For many families this becomes a very delicate balancing act: providing their kids with enough emotional and material support to make their childhood fun and enriching, while at the same time providing opportunities for their children to develop the self-esteem, moral compass, self-discipline and work ethic necessary for them to lead happy, healthy, and fulfilling lives.

So what is a parent's primary responsibility? In essence I believe it is to prepare their children to be powerful forces for good in the community at large, to prepare them to be successful in such a way that the greatest number of people benefit. No longer is it good enough simply to make sure they achieve material success. Many of the problems we face today are a result of people looking at the world as a place of finite resources, committed to accruing as much as they can for themselves, regardless of the cost to others. If we are to raise our children well, we must raise them to see resources as more or less unlimited; to consider how they can do the most good for the most people. We do not live in a zero-sum universe. We live in one in which all can prosper!

In order to meet this responsibility one of your most important tasks is to help your children grow their brains. We have to help them develop the ability to understand the long-term consequences of the choices they make. How do we do this? We do this by imitating the real world . . . safely.

Letting Kids Fail

There are three kinds of men. The one that learns by reading. The few who learn by observation. The rest of them have to pee on the electric fence for themselves.

Will Rogers

The world is an amazing place. It is thrilling. It is wonderful. It is beautiful. And it is dangerous. It is a place where one can experience great sadness and great joy. It is a place where failure and success are equally available. As adults we get to experience much of what the world has to offer . . . and if we are up to the task and pay attention, we get to cause much of what we experience.

Children also get to experience much of what the world has to offer though, if all goes well, on a smaller scale. Children will also get to learn how to cause their experiences if there is someone there to teach them. Your role as a parent is to safely guide them through these experiences. If you are to prepare your children well, you cannot hide them from these experiences, you must guide them through these experiences . . . and if you know how, teach them how to cause their experiences. Not only can you teach them how to navigate, you can teach them how to set their own course.

The sooner your son learns that actions have consequences, the sooner your son will have experiences he can learn to navigate through. As he learns the costs associated with some behaviors and the rewards associated with others, he will begin to connect his actions to consequences. Having made these connections he can then learn how to best respond to such costs and rewards.

In our society we have begun putting way too much attention on attempting to insulate our children from negative experiences rather than teaching them how to understand those experiences and how to use those experiences to their advantage. On the playing field no longer do young children get an opportunity to learn how to win, or find the wins in losing . . . we don't keep score, and everyone gets ribbons. Perhaps this is not so much an attempt to insulate our children as it is an attempt to insulate their parents. The number of parents losing all perspective around their kid's athletic events seems to be climbing.

More importantly, in the classroom, far too many parents are loath to have their kids receive poor grades. Rather than receive poor grades, parents are more than willing to go far beyond helping their kids to their schoolwork. Moms and dads are doing it themselves. Recently, I was talking with a principal at a private school in Portland, Oregon. She was telling me how they no longer give out awards at their annual science fair because the school staff tired of rewarding the efforts of parents.

I was working with a seventh grader who had a biography project to do. This was an important project, it was worth many points, and was going to be a significant part of his grade. I helped him choose his topic and organize his thoughts. A few weeks later when I went to his home his parents proudly showed me the work that the family had done on the boy's assignment. It was tremendous work. It looked good enough for National Geographic, and certainly was not the work of my student, their son.

And if parents are not doing a substantial portion of the work themselves, they are doing everything in their power to make sure the work gets done on time. Parents keep track of their children's work, know when it's due, consistently remind them to get it done on time, and make sure they bring their work to school.

I'm sure parents believe they're helping. They likely believe that if they stay on top of their children when they are young, they will develop good work habits in time. Unfortunately this only works up to a point. If parents are still doing this through junior high school, they are very misguided. Instead of developing good work habits, students develop a reliance on their parents, a reliance that hurts them in high school and beyond.

Couple this with well-meaning middle school teachers who give their students many opportunities to make up work and turn it in late, and you have a recipe for disaster in the freshman year of high school. If students get into the habit of turning in work late and being allowed to make up work at the end of the term during junior high school, they can be in for a rude awakening in high school where many teachers allow no such thing.

If you want to help your child learn to take care of their own business, you must give them the opportunity to do so and let them fail if they do not. The best time to start providing them with such opportunities is in middle school. Elementary school is the time for children to learn how to work and a parent helping their children remember their projects and homework is a good thing. High school is when grades count, and because they count it is not the best time for kids to learn the lessons necessary to become self-sufficient. Junior high school, on the other hand, is an optimal time for them to learn these lessons. Grades do not count near as much, and the long-term costs of failure are quite small.

So, junior high school is a great time for parents to really imitate the workings of the world. This is a time you can truly make a significant difference . . . and this is how you do it. First, sit down with your son or daughter and be very clear about your expectations. These expectations should not only be limited to their school performance; they should include their behavior at home, the level of cooperation you require and how they comport themselves in the community. Keep these discussions light and work toward building understanding and agreement.

Discuss passing on greater responsibility for their work to them and work out a good pace to do so. Then, sit back, watch, and see how they do. Check on them, be supportive, see if they need or want any help, and help them out. If they're taking care of business, great! Simply continue to keep an eye on them. If at some point they are not taking care of business, sit down with them and discuss fair consequences. Once you agree upon fair consequences, and you, the parents, are the final arbiters of what is fair, make those consequences stick. Preferably, do this as best you can without being pejorative. Be as matter-of-fact as you can be.

If the consequence for not turning in an assignment is no gaming on the computer, be detached and calm as you follow through. If the consequence for not doing the dishes is no cell phone for the evening, hold your position. Remember, you are imitating the real world. The real world cares not a whit if a person succeeds or fails. The consequences automatically are meted out. Do your best to do the same. In this way your child will have a better chance of connecting behaviors to consequences.

This will take some extra work on your part. You're going to have to be in contact with your child's teachers and proactively learn whether his or her assignments are being turned in on time. Most teachers will be only too happy to help you out.

By the way, the same is true with rewards. If you're going to set up a consequence structure you should also set up a reward structure. The key is consistent follow-up. This is the work you as parents need to do to help your kids become more functional and to give them the best chance to succeed in high school and college.

Some time ago a number of us were having a discussion. My friend's wife was bemoaning the fact that her four-year-old daughter always immediately minds her father and rarely obeys her without much repetition. A friend of ours who is a psychologist looked at her daughter and asked her:

"When your daddy tells you to do something does he mean it?"

"Yes."

I'm sure you can guess what the next question was,

"When your mommy tells you to do something does she mean it?"

"No," was her simple, straightforward answer.

Our friend just looked at the mom with raised eyebrows and shrugged his shoulders. That was all that needed to be said. We all learn from a very young age who means it and who doesn't and we respond accordingly.

The better you mimic the real world, the better prepared your sons and daughters will be to interact with it. With clear communication between all members of your family this can actually go quite smoothly with everyone benefiting. At first your kids may resist, but if you stick to your guns and hold your position, in time they will learn that compliance works best. Once they have developed their ability to take care of their own business they will love and thank you the rest of their lives for teaching them how.

Metamorphosis: Transitioning from Kid to Adult

Human beings are the only creatures that allow their children to come back home.

Bill Cosby

Parents would do well to endeavor to raise their children to be their friends. This does not mean treating them as friends when they are still children; it means that when they finally become full-fledged adults our relationships become less parent-child, and more friend to friend. I remember how cool it was growing older, hanging out with my parents, and simply talking adult to adult about whatever the topic of the day was. I remember our sharing ideas, laughs, and the occasional off-color joke.

However, I don't remember the exact moment I became an adult; there likely wasn't just one. I do, however, remember much of the transition, in particular the shift in my parents' minds when they began to consider me grown up. Over the years I've identified three markers that indicate graduation to adulthood. Teaching kids what these signposts are can only help to speed them on their way.

Before I start, let me say that growing into adulthood is not automatic nor is it age dependent. Having the right to drive, vote, and drink does not make one an adult. Growing older is no guarantee of reaching adulthood. I have known 16-year-olds who are more adult than some 60-year-olds. There are those who never quite make it, though thankfully the vast majority of us do.

Taking Responsibility

The first of these markers is taking responsibility. I do not limit taking responsibility to your actions. Fully realized adults take responsibility for their attitudes, thoughts, and feelings, as well as their actions, and all the concomitant consequences. When people are being children they lie, blame others, and/or do what they can to avoid experiencing the consequences of their creations; not unlike a five-year-old getting caught in the cookie jar before lunch.

"Are you eating a cookie?"

The little girl shakes her head, "No," while trying to swallow the cookie as fast as she can.

I remember fighting with my younger brother quite frequently and asserting it was his fault every time we were caught. As a 12-year-old I remember ditching religious services, getting busted, and making up the most far-fetched story in the hopes that my father would buy it and not severely punish me. Totally kid stuff.

We become adults when we become willing and able to be accountable and responsible, then gracefully take what comes. I know one family who, like many others, use timeouts and the removal of toys to discipline their children. One afternoon my friend's two-and-a-half years old daughter went to her mother with her favorite video in hand, gave it to her, and said, "Mommy, I'm about to be bad." This was a very adult thing to do. Of course the parents were both somewhat troubled and at the same time quite proud.

I tell my students that if there is something they want to do that they know their parents will not approve of, think carefully and determine if doing this thing is worth the consequence your parents will dish out. If going to that party is worth being grounded for a month, do it if you must, then tell your parents and accept the consequence of your action with a smile. The first part is easy; it's accepting the consequences with a smile that's the tough part for a kid.

If taking responsibility for our actions is difficult, taking responsibility for our thoughts and feelings can be much, much more so. Your thoughts and your feelings are your own. People do not **make** us feel certain ways nor do they **make** us think certain ways, no matter how much it may seem otherwise. Yes, we can influence how other people think and feel and they can influence us, and we certainly must teach our children to be responsible for their influences, but at the end of the day our feelings and thoughts are ultimately our responsibility. If we can impart this to our children they will be infinitely better off and they will be at huge advantage throughout their lives.

It is nigh impossible for me to put a number on the amount of times my mother said, "You make me so angry," or "You hurt me," or "Why do you have to embarrass me so?" or something to that effect. I am sure you have had someone in your life say something similar to you many times over. The truth is, whether my mom was aware of it or not, it was her approach to be angry, hurt, or embarrassed. My mother had the option to respond to what I did in a myriad of ways . . . and she chose those.

This is perhaps the hardest thing I discuss for people to accept. Truth be told, almost no one does; but acceptance or rejection doesn't change the truth of it. We humans are constantly trying to sell others on the idea that our feelings are their fault. This is certainly 'normal' yet there is a serious downside to this viewpoint. You see, what we sell we are obligated to buy. So, when others accuse us of hurting their feelings, embarrassing them, making them mad, we are obligated to take them seriously and so we can become more inhibited. And the more inhibited we become, the less successful we are able to be.

We are much better off learning to create and control our own thoughts and feelings, then teaching our children to do the same. In this way they will have the tools to become more responsible individuals. How do you learn how to do this? I'll give you some tools in chapter five.

There are other important reasons for us to be as responsible as we can for our own outcomes. How many times have you heard students blame teachers for their poor performance? How many times have you heard teachers blame students and their parents for their students' poor performance? How many times have you heard parents blame teachers and the school for the poor performance of their daughters and sons?

Certainly a case can be made for each of these viewpoints. However, difficulty arises when we try to do something about it, for putting the responsibility in another's hands leaves us impotent . . . and that is not a good place to be left. After all, if it's the teacher's fault, what can your daughter really do? Taking responsibility for their results, regardless of the circumstances, at least gives your child a chance to improve their situation. More often than not it gives them a great chance, and as they improve their situations, so they improve their self-efficacy.

Working First

All the activities in our lives can be placed in one of three categories: we work, we play, and we rest. These three general activities must be balanced if we are to lead happy, healthy, and fulfilling lives. We all know what happens when we work so much we have little time for anything else . . . burnout. We also know what it feels like when we have not worked enough, when we have spent too much time playing . . . a certain feeling of ennui and inadequacy. Finally, most of us have experienced the lethargy, that lack of energy from getting too much rest.

Before we go too much farther, let's define our terms and make sure we are all on the same page. Let's start with work. Work often gets a bad rap. When I've asked people to define work they often define it in very unappealing terms.

"Work is something we have to do."

"Work is what pays the bills."

"Work is what we do so we can have fun."

Think about what work means to you. It's no wonder our attitudes towards work are sometimes less than enthusiastic.

The actual definition of work is: energy expended towards the accomplishment of a goal. For an activity to be 'work' we have to engage in it with a goal in mind. If you're not aware of what you're trying to accomplish with your activity, you're really not working . . . you're just expending energy. So, it's important that your kids learn the difference between expending energy with no particular end in mind and work. They will be much more likely to do work when they are aware of the goal they are working to accomplish. More importantly, they will be more likely to enjoy the work they're doing.

We seem to have a better understanding of play. Essentially, play is activities we engage in for amusement. Play does not involve the pursuit of a goal other than the goals of enjoying what we're doing and winning whatever game we're playing. If we have a goal beyond the winning of the game or the enjoyment of the experience, we are actually not playing we are working. It is certainly possible for work to feel like play; in fact this is quite desirable. However, if play feels like work it is no longer play. The young athlete who is working on her soccer game so she can get a scholarship is no longer 'playing' soccer. Time and time again young athletes, young musicians, young performers give up these activities because they're no longer fun, no longer play. For many of these young people it is only after they have set aside their goals that they can recapture the sheer joy of participating.

The last of our triumvirate is rest. Rest is refreshing ease or inactivity after exertion or labor. In America we seem to have become pretty good at working and playing and not nearly as good at resting. Too many of us do not get the rest we need. I've actually heard people say they get rest by going to the gym. I know people who never take time to simply do nothing, to just hang out around peacefully and relax. And we all certainly know people who don't get enough sleep. If we are to have plenty of energy for working and playing, we must get the right amount of rest.

When we are very young play comes first. When we get through playing we rest, and we don't seem to like working very much. As parents we learn to make work seem like play for our younger children. This is how we get them to do things. As youngsters become teenagers they accept work as part of daily life, but most young teenagers still much prefer to play and will work only when they have to. For these teenagers play remains their priority followed by work and rest.

One of the major signs that a person is evolving into an adult is that work has moved to the head of the list. Adults work first, then play, and then rest. If we have designed our lives well our work actually feels like play and we thoroughly enjoy doing it. Most of us at least have figured out how to take some enjoyment from our work. The more we can do this, the better. Whether or not we enjoy all the aspects of our work, we do take care of business first. When we've taken care of enough business we go out and play, and if we are smart we get enough rest so we can do it all over again.

I have had the opportunity to watch teenagers struggle putting work first as they transition to adulthood. For most, the struggle abates and the transition happens somewhere in their junior or senior year. In the best of cases the parents have a clear understanding of work and teach their kids from a very young age to enjoy the sense of accomplishment that comes from work well done. Of course, even with the best parenting, under the best circumstances, when our kids hit puberty it can be a bit of a crapshoot for a while.

Hormones or no, the sooner that kids establish the habit of taking care of business first, the sooner they will be successful.

Those that do establish the habit tend to enjoy school more, enjoy being with their families and friends more, and in general enjoy their lives more.

Paying Your Own Way

The third marker on the journey to becoming an adult is paying your own way. A person is not an adult unless they are financially taking care of themselves. Of course we cannot and should not expect teenagers to be footing the bill for their existence. For most people these days we don't expect them to do this until they're in their early 20s, after they're finished with their education. I guess we expect them to get there a little earlier if they go right into the workforce out of high school.

We can, however, begin their training before they leave the house. Teenagers who work have a leg up on their peers in this regard. Being exposed to the work world at a young age has its advantages. Teenagers can find themselves in environments that are stimulating and focusing. A young lady may find herself helping out a mechanic and discovering she has an aptitude for working on cars. The young man who thought he had an interest in the law might help out in a law office and come to realize it's not the kind of work he thought it was.

My friend's son, a high school junior who was not as focused as he might be on his education, got a summer internship in a field in which he was quite interested. He expected to be doing actual work in the field; instead all he got to do was some clerical work which he found uninteresting; he didn't enjoy the experience as much as he thought he would. Still, he did a great job and, at the same time, learned about the kind of work that is available for people with limited skills and education. I hope his focus on his education has been renewed.

There is a natural urge in kids to want to grow up. At their cores girls want to be women and boys, men. Even though there are times they all wish to stay children, these times come and go rapidly. The urge to be adults remains primordially powerful. Taking responsibility for oneself, working first, and paying your own way, are the chief markers on the road to adulthood. Knowing these guideposts can greatly benefit our kids. It is up to all of us to help them along their path.

Building Self-Esteem

It can't be emphasized enough that healthy self-esteem is critical to enjoying a wonderful life. Parents play a colossal role in their children's self-esteem development. Self-esteem is something very special It is different, though connected to, self-confidence, self-efficacy, and self-concept. Self-esteem is literally self value; it is the value we put on ourselves. It is a measure of our value to our families, friends, and community.

Self-esteem also has a significant objective component to it, for regardless of what we believe our value to be, we can actually see evidence of it. How much do we help? How much better do people get as a result of interacting with us? How much does life improve around us? These are the actual measures of self-esteem.

To help your child develop their self-esteem you have to provide them with opportunities to be valuable. However, this is not enough. You also have to help them be aware that they are, in fact, being valuable. For a child to develop healthy self-esteem they need to do things that are valuable as well as be aware of the value they are producing.

Doing this is quite straightforward. From a very young age, it can be as early as about 18 months, provide your child with opportunities to be of service. For instance, when they're that young just asking them to pick up something off the floor and handing it to you is plenty. Then, when they help you, validate them and thank them for helping you. As they get older putting away their toys, helping clean their room, helping with their baby sister are all opportunities for them to be of value. Make sure you let them know how helpful they are being.

As they get older provide them with more and more meaningful opportunities. Ask them to create ways they could contribute to the family and their community, encourage them to do so, and help them be aware of the value they produce. The more value they create and the more they are aware of what they have done, the more self-esteem they will develop. This is how you develop actual self-esteem.

I want to emphasize that it is of great importance that your children's self-esteem be grounded in actuality. It is important that as they get older they can see the value they are responsible for producing. This is very different from telling kids how wonderful they are. Telling kids they're great is certainly a good thing to do; it helps build their self-confidence.

Self-esteem is different. If we simply tell our children how valuable they are without having them demonstrate it, we're likely to produce people who believe they are more valuable than they actually are, with a sense of unearned entitlement. If, on the other hand, our children are not aware of the value they contribute, they are likely to grow up believing they are worth less than they in fact are. It is incumbent upon parents to help their children develop a healthy, accurate assessment of their self-worth. By providing them with quality opportunities and awareness we can go a long way to ensuring they have wonderful, satisfying lives.

Student Interlude

Your Junior Moment

An Open Letter to Freshmen and Sophomores

If you are reading this it's most likely because your mom or dad think you need to. That could be strike one against you really thinking about what you're about to read. Most of you don't who I am. That could be strike two. A few of you have more important things to do. That could be strike three. Be this as it may, all I'm asking is for a few minutes of your time to read and consider.

In a year or two you will all be juniors and during your junior year you will come upon a very interesting moment. It's a moment almost every student will confront, like it or not. It has nothing to do with your parents, teachers or any other adult for that matter. For many students this moment is the beginning of much happiness and excitement; for many others it's the beginning of much disappointment and dejection. I have worked with hundreds and hundreds of students over the past 12 years and this moment always comes. It is the moment when a student seriously begins preparing to go to college.

For those students who took care of business during the first two years of high school it's a time filled with options. For those students who blew off their first year or two it's a moment that is often filled with fear and regret. I cannot begin to tell you what it's like when that moment comes and you realize you are not eligible to go to the

71

four year universities that interest you because your GPA is too low . . . and the only reason your GPA is too low is because you goofed off during freshman and/or sophomore year.

Now it's one thing to have really given school your best shot and not done well; after all, school is not for everyone. Students who give it there best have a certain sense of satisfaction with their effort. However, it's an entirely different experience knowing the only reason you're not going to enjoy one of the best experiences of your young life is because you were lazy or more interested in hanging out with your friends, or playing video games, or simply found school boring. If this is the case you will likely get a sick feeling of regret in the pit of your stomach.

If you are one these students it's an incredibly harsh time. After all, you have assumed you'll be going to college since you were young. It's a very rude awakening to find out that you're not. Oh, of course you can go eventually if you want. You can go to a community college for two years then transfer to a four year college, but that is not what you have in mind. Am I right? I cannot begin to tell you how many juniors and seniors I have worked with who messed up their first year or two and feel awful. While their friends were deciding whether to study business and snowboard at the University of Colorado, study medicine and sail at UCLA or study anthropology and surf at the University of Hawaii, they no longer realistically had those options.

So please do not assume college is automatic. It is not. You have to take care of business. It really will not take much for most of you to be successful, especially if this is your freshman year. The next time you come home from school just do your homework before you start making phone calls or getting on the computer. Pay attention in class. If you don't understand something, ask for help.

Whether you like it or not, that moment in your junior year is coming. It is up to you and you alone to make sure that moment is a good one.

Part 2

The New Fundamentals

We cannot always build the future for our youth, but we can build our youth for the future

Franklin D. Roosevelt

Optimism is true moral courage.

Earnest Shackleton

Chapter Five

Attitude Rules

Carefully watch your thoughts, for they become your words. Manage and watch your words, for they will become your actions. Consider and judge your actions for they have become your habits. Acknowledge and watch your habits, for they shall become your values. Understand and embrace your values, for they become your destiny.

Mohandas Gandhi

Attitude rules! Our attitude is the state from which our thoughts, feelings, perceptions, actions, and reactions all flow. Our attitudes determine what opportunities we will notice, what judgments we will make, what goals we will set. Attitudes are powerful. They can determine what we believe we can and cannot do. They are the most important factors in determining the quality of life we will experience.

Have you ever awakened on the "wrong side" of the bed? Of course you have. So have we all. You know what happens when you wake up this way. You're grouchy, grumbly, and irritable. Things that don't ordinarily get to you, tweak you. Things that would normally irk you a little bit bother you a whole lot. You've also awakened on the "right side" of the bed. You're optimistic. Things that might ordinarily annoy you roll off you like water off a duck's back. There isn't a problem you can't solve. All is right with the world.

The real difference between these two experiences of your day is your attitude. Many years ago while I was a graduate student at UCLA a friend and I were having breakfast. My friend was disturbed about something; he had woken up on the wrong side of the bed. During breakfast I was able to help him gain some perspective and lighten his mood. As we parted company he was feeling much better. When we saw each other later that day he thanked me because just after we parted that morning he noticed a beautiful young woman sitting outside the music building. He told me that being in his more normal upbeat state he introduced himself to her, had a lovely conversation, and had set a date up with her for that night. That afternoon he told me he was pretty sure if he was feeling the way he was feeling in the morning there is no way he would've approached her. Change in attitude . . . change in life.

We all have experience seeing our attitudes at work. We have all experienced being at their mercy, being in a bad mood and watching events around us going from bad to worse, and so putting us in a worse mood. We've all also experienced the opposite; being in a good mood and watching things get better and better. This is called being the effect, and we all know what being the effect is like. "Obey your thirst!" Be the effect of your urges. This is the predominant message out there. Being the effect is good for business.

What many of us seem to be unaware of is that we can also be the cause of our attitudes. We are not taught this in school, there are no public service announcements on television, and I don't know about you, but I don't recall my parents ever teaching me this. Be that as it may, we can cause our attitudes. We can go to bed and determine what attitude we will wake up with. We can notice we have a bad attitude and change it to an attitude we prefer on the spot. We can do this because we are human; it is one of our God-given capacities. We can all learn how to do this and we can teach our daughters and sons to do the same.

Understanding Attitude

Taking our cue from the levels of learning, let's first clearly understand what attitudes are, how we get them, and how they work. Our attitudes are our approaches to the world. They are our state of being, our mental/emotional state. They are our outlooks on life. Think of it like an airplane. An airplane has to have a certain attitude if it is to land safely. If the plane approaches the runway too steeply it will crash, too shallow it will miss the runway. It has to have the right attitude, approach, in order to safely make it to the ground. Similarly, if we are to be successful with what we are engaged in, we have to have an approach, an attitude that will work.

At one time or another, your son or daughter has approached a task, be it a homework assignment or a chore around the house, with an attitude of conflict or rebellion . . . you know, the 'I'm going to hate this' look. From here things almost never go as well as they can. S/he is likely to make mistakes. The task usually takes two or three times longer to accomplish than it needs to. When your child approaches the same task with an attitude of easy focus everything tends to go much better, they get their work done quicker and with greater accuracy. Not to mention, they're so much more fun to be around.

Our attitudes act as filters on our perceptions. We are all familiar with the saying, 'Pessimists see the glass as half-empty. Optimists see the glass as half-full.' It is much deeper than that. People who are pessimistic not only see the glass half empty, they expect the glass to be empty, they look for empty glasses, they do not truly believe glasses can be full. When a full glass is put in front of them they may not even see it, they may even 'accidentally' knock it over. When a person is being pessimistic they look for things to go wrong, and in the looking for things to go wrong, they often cause them to do so.

An optimist, on the other hand, expects glasses to be full, they look for full glasses, they believe glasses can be full. Upon seeing the full glass they drink from it. When a person is being optimistic they look for things to go right, for them to work, and in the looking for things to go right, they often cause them to do so.

For example, take Susan and Maria. Today Susan is being rebellious; she is a bit angry. To Susan it seems like the world is against her. At work her boss, not in a great mood herself, asks Susan to do something for her. Susan, with that certain chip on her shoulder, makes some unfortunate comment a bit too audibly, not quite under her breath, takes the assignment and begins to walk away. On another day her boss may have let it slide, but today she challenges Susan and an exchange takes place that neither Susan nor her boss enjoy.

Maria works in the same office as Susan and is feeling good today. She is upbeat and has a kind word for everybody in the office. The boss, in an even worse mood, in part due to her confrontation with Susan, asks Maria to do something for her. Maria cheerfully accepts the assignment and Maria's cheerfulness has the effect of putting her boss a little more ease. The following month a promotion opens up requiring closer work with the boss. Guess who gets it? You can bet that if Susan hasn't changed her tune she will likely be blaming that 'kiss up Maria' and that 'incompetent boss' for her not getting promoted.

This is one example of our attitudes affecting our outcomes. Scenes like this can be repeated dozens of times a day in our lives. Often we may never know the true consequences. Even the smallest of our actions can begin a cascade of effects. That you are happy and complemented the gentleman at the checkout counter in your local supermarket may have helped put him in a better mood than he is used to. Upon getting home he feels so good he takes his son out to the park. At the park he and his son see an older man in distress and help him out. To show his gratitude the older man offers to set the grocery store clerk up with a better job and better pay. All because you complimented him. You will never know.

Our attitudes also exert their influence when it comes to goal setting. Our attitudes strongly inform what goals we consider possible for ourselves. Those with negative attitudes are much less likely to set fulfilling goals for themselves simply because they do not believe they can accomplish them. This is such a handicap for people wanting to lead good lives. Conversely, challenging, rewarding goals are quite available to those with positive attitudes for they are confident in their ability and expect to succeed. Our attitudes are powerfully influential.

Basic and Specific Attitudes

Remember, our attitudes are our approaches to our world. Having a poor attitude simply means our approach likely will not bring us what we want; having a good attitude means that our approach likely will bring us what we want. At any given time there are two classes of attitudes we need to consider: basic and specific. Basic attitudes are the attitudes we generally have as we move through our day. We all have two of them: the attitude we adopt when we believe things are not going our way and the attitude we adopt when we believe things are going well. A person might become fearful when she takes a few hits and more focused as she experiences some success. Another person might approach his day in a state of conflict when events go against him and he might get careless when events are to his liking.

Specific attitudes are context dependent. All of us have weaknesses and strengths, we all have areas of our lives which we are better at than others. We all know people who are wonderful family members and at the same time clueless about making money. We all know people who are brilliant at making money yet not so much so when it comes to making friends. Generally speaking, in the areas in which we're not good we have poor attitudes and in the areas in which we excel we have very good attitudes.

So why do some people have bad attitudes and others have good ones? Why are some people pessimists and others optimists? Where do our attitudes come from?

How Attitudes Arise

For the most part our attitudes develop below our awareness. Our attitudes are by and large a result of the stresses we've experienced and the successes we have had in our lives. The more the stress, the worse our attitudes. The more the success the better our attitudes. If we have experienced a fair amount of stress in our relationships, it is less likely that we will have attitudes, approaches to relationships that will get us where we want to go. Similarly, if we have experienced a fair amount of financial success it is more likely that we will have attitudes, approaches to money that will get us to our destination.

Where all this attitude development starts is in our childhood. If our parents had a lot of success with the family finances, it is very likely we will have healthy outlooks regarding money. If our parents created a warm and loving household, it is very likely we will have healthy outlooks regarding family.

This being said, what we experienced as children does not etch our attitudes in stone; we have many experiences outside our families. More importantly, we may have learned how to determine them ourselves. However, our childhood does get us started.

Another group of inputs that have significant impact on the development of our attitudes is the media. What we see is what we get. This is a discussion I have with almost every student with whom I work. The music we listen to, the news we pay attention to, the books and periodicals we read, the television and movies we watch all contribute to the formation of our attitudes. If most of the music your son listens to deals with violence, loss, death, and nihilism don't be surprised if he finds himself thinking that the world is not a fun place. If the books and periodicals your daughter reads are predominantly about grim people and events, don't be surprised if she finds herself feeling a little depressed. If the preponderance of your child's television and movie viewing deals with dysfunctional people behaving dysfunctionally, don't be surprised if they find themselves taking a dim view of their fellow human. As they say in the world of computer programming, 'garbage in, garbage out.'

Some time ago my cousin, who was 15 at the time, told me he watched Pink Floyd's "The Wall" every day for a month. For those of you not familiar with the movie, it's filled with dark imagery set to the band's music. When I asked him how this went, he told me he found himself feeling a little depressed. He said it was a really good experiment; he learned the impact of music and movies on his psyche. My wish is that all young men and women learn the same lesson.

If we have gained clarity as to what our attitudes are, how they come to be, how they filter our perceptions and influence our behaviors, we can move on to the next stage of learning, becoming capable with our own attitudes. It is time to begin to learn how to create and maintain the attitudes that will serve us best, and teach our daughters and sons how to do so as well.

Taking Control

We can be the ones to determine our own mental/emotional states of being, our own outlooks, our own attitudes . . . and we can help our children develop their own capacity to do the same.

Our understanding of attitudes will point the way. Before we get into it you will notice that the skills and exercises I am outlining are for both you and your children. I do this because your attitudes strongly influence your children's attitudes, especially when they're young. So the more you approach the world in ways that work for you, the greater the likelihood that your kids will do so.

Reduce Stress / Increase Success

> *Time flies like the wind. Fruit flies like bananas.*
>
> Grouch Marx

Our attitudes are a function of the stress we have experienced and the successes we have had in our lives. Two obvious ways you can improve your attitudes are to reduce your stress and increase your success. "Sure, easy for you to say," I hear some of you thinking to yourselves. Well, yes it is actually easy for me to say. And it's really not all that difficult for you to accomplish.

Let's look at reducing stress. First, do you experience more stress than you would like? If the answer is yes, what can you do to make your life a little easier? Could you cut one thing out of your schedule? Could you go to bed a little earlier one night or wake up a little later one morning? Could you get a massage? What could you do to put a little more ease into your life? Could you exercise a little more? Could you take a little more time for yourself? Could you have a little more play time with your kids? Could you take a walk with your loved ones? Could you laugh a little more?

You've probably noticed the repeated word in almost all these questions: little. One of the tricks to making your life easier is to make changes in small increments. A common mistake many people make is considering and committing to sweeping change. For most of us sweeping changes are not only unrealistic they can be fairly stressful to pursue. It is often wiser to bite off smaller more manageable chunks. You may find that even the smallest of changes can have immense impacts on your life.

Once you are moving in the direction that's right for you, you can get to work on your kids. How can you make your children's lives easier? I think what you will notice right off the bat is that easing your life will naturally make your children's life easier. The happier the parents are, the happier the kids.

Certainly, if your kids are overscheduled you can reduce their load; give them more free play time. Just to be clear here, I do not suggest reducing their load by giving them less chores to do or a free pass on some school assignment. I am suggesting that if you have your kid signed up to participate in two sports, the Science Olympiad, and music lessons you may want to rein some of that back. If you are the type of parent who pushes your kids to perform, you may want to reassess your efforts. Now I am the last one who believes in taking it easy on kids; however, there is often a fine line between pushing hard enough to help them develop the strength they will need to be successful and pushing them too hard. In the end you know your kids better than anyone else, so this is for you to judge.

Let's take a look at increasing success. Sometimes increasing success is as simple as noticing when you have been successful. We often do a whole lot throughout our daily lives that we take for granted. My father is an example. He was a good man. To me he was a great man. Oh, he never achieved any fame or notoriety; only his family, his friends and those he worked with knew who he was. He had a smile and a kind word for everyone he met; he would give you the shirt off his back. If upon entering your home he noticed your door squeaking, he'd look for a screwdriver and some WD-40 and fix it for you.

My dad raised three boys to be good men, (I might be a little biased on this last point.) and took care of my mother, his wife of more than 40 years. Regretfully, my dad always believed he was lacking, that what he did was never good enough. You see, dad never made a lot of money and felt he didn't provide adequately for his family. However, by the time he retired he had saved enough money for him and my mother to live fairly comfortably through their remaining years.

In his mid-seventies he contracted Parkinson's disease. Towards the end of his life he required around the clock care. Fortunately, he had the foresight and the means to be cared for at home. Unfortunately, towards the very end, this was inadequate and he was going to have to go into a nursing home. My father knew that this option would eat away most of the retirement funds and leave my mother with precious little. So, instead of going into a nursing home, my father stopped eating, stopped drinking, and stopped taking any medication. He died on the holiest day of the Jewish year. Not bad for an Orthodox Jewish man. I hope he passed with an appreciation for how much he accomplished.

Simply being aware of all the good you do will increase the amount of successes in your tally. If you look upon your life and do not notice enough success, wake up every day with the intention of making someone's life a little better. Think of little things you can do to improve the lives of your family. Think of little things you can do to make the lives of the people with whom you work just a little easier. Then do some of these. Keep a log of who you helped and what you did. It goes without saying that you should enter all the successes you have had in pursuit of your own goals into your log, too. I guarantee you'll feel better and better about yourself as your tally rises; and as your tally climbs so will your attitude.

You can do the same with your children. Help them notice all the good things they do every day. Teach them to plan to make others' days a little better and teach them to keep track of all the help they provide. Of course, remember to give them plenty of hugs and kisses, praise and acknowledgment for the work they do to improve their part of world.

Provide them with opportunities to have many successes for themselves. Helping them set goals for themselves and helping them notice their accomplishments is a good way to help them build up their storehouse of wins. Speaking of wins, you can go a long way towards making sure they know how to find the wins in every game they play regardless of the outcome simply by asking them what went right, what they did well. Did they improve from the last time they played? Did they support their teammates? Did they have fun? That old adage still holds true: it really is not whether you win or lose, it is how you play the game . . . and if you play the game well, with the attitude you wish to exhibit . . . you win big.

Use Your Imagination

How do you know if you could use an attitude adjustment? Ask yourself, **"Are there aspects of my life that are not going well enough for me or that could use some improvement. If so, what are they?"**

Make sure you name the areas. The answers are the areas where improving your attitude would help. Once you have identified an area ask yourself, **"What attitude would work best here?"** and explore different attitudes. Sometimes your exploration can be improved with a thesaurus and dictionary. We often find we do not have the right label for the attitude we wish to emanate. A dictionary and thesaurus are great tools for expanding our attitudinal vocabulary.

For example, let's say you think the attitude you wish to take on is 'happiness,' but this just doesn't quite hit it on the head. Go to your thesaurus and look up the word 'happiness' or 'happy,' and you will find a number of words that are similar yet not exactly the same. Perhaps 'joyful' resonates with you more. Perhaps 'glad.' Perhaps 'blessed,' 'cheerful,' 'ecstatic,' 'pleased,' 'playful,' 'tickled,' 'delighted,' or' blissful' better describes what you're after.

This exploration can be much fun; it can also be quite enlightening. Take the time to look up your words in the dictionary. You'll get a deeper understanding of the word's meaning and a better feel for identifying if it's the one that is most true for you at this time.

Once you have the word representing the attitude you want you can ask yourself, **"What would it be like to operate with this attitude?" "What would I be doing differently?"** In this way you begin using your imagination to explore what your world would be like if you approached it from this attitude. As you explore you will notice your attitude beginning to change. The more full your exploration, the more your attitude will shift to the one you want. Imagine yourself going through your entire day with the attitude of your choice . . . then go out and do it. You may want to leave reminders for yourself on your refrigerator, in your bathroom, in your car, on your desk. Whatever you need to do to increase the likelihood of success. Do it and see what happens.

One time a number of us were sparring in our martial arts class. After we had gone at it for about 15 minutes my instructor stopped us and asked to us to imagine we were 900-year-old martial arts masters who had been successful in tens of thousands of engagements. He had us close our eyes and get the feel for what that would be like. Then he had us spar again. The difference was marked. We all became quieter, more measured, and more direct in our attacks. We were all immediately better than we had been 10 minutes earlier.

As you practice this you will become more capable, and as your confidence rises you can begin training your kids. When your kids are young you can turn this into a game. You can choose different attitudes from which to perform certain activities. We can put away our toys happily, fold our clothes easily, and play on the computer with confidence. In this way your children will learn that attitude can be a choice.

Recall Exercise (Samuels)

The Recall Exercise is a variation on the above approach and is quite simple. This exercise begins the same way, identifying an attitude or state you wish to create. This time instead of imagining what it would be like to operate from the state, simply, **"Recall a time you experienced (fill in the state of your choice.)"** Continue recalling times you experienced that state until your state improves.

Feel free to recall many different times you experienced the state of your choice or simply recall one or two times you experienced the state of your choice repeatedly. If you can't recall any, and this does happen once in a while, feel free to make some up. Your mind doesn't really know the difference. You may need to recall ten, twenty, or more individual events for your attitude to shift. Or you may need to recall the same event ten, twenty, or more times to get the shift you desire. More often than not though, it only takes a few repitions.

This is quite a versatile exercise. If you notice your daughter is frustrated with her math homework, you can ask her to remember when she did well in math. Doing this just a few times is often all she will need to get back on track. If your son is getting down on himself at basketball practice, having him recall times he was successful will often turn his attitude right around.

WINS (Samuels)

As discussed earlier, our attitudes are a function of the amount of stress we've experienced and the amount of success we've enjoyed. Wouldn't it be great if there was a way to increase the number of our successes? For by increasing our successes we would elevate our attitude. WINS is an exercise that does just that. Additionally, this exercise takes advantage of the power of our imagination that we talked about on the previous pages.

WINS is perhaps the most powerful exercise presented in this book. If your children learn this exercise and practice it on a consistent basis, I guarantee you that their attitudes will improve and their odds for success will rise. They will become more self-confident and develop greater self-esteem. If this exercise is done diligently, over time they will become more and more aware of what they are actually capable of.

WINS is an acronym that represents the four questions that comprise the exercise:

W: What did you **W**in at yesterday?
 I: What **I**mprovements could you make?
N: What will your **N**ext wins be?
S: If all this went well what **S**tate would you be in?

This exercise works best if the answers to these questions are written down. I suggest providing your daughter or son a journal book or a spiral notebook that they will use to keep track of their progress. Any book that has contained, fixed pages will do. Basically, anything other than a three ring binder in which the expectation is that you will add and remove pages. Get together with your child and find something that they feel is cool to write in.

Title each page at the top: WINS, and make sure each page is dated. Dating each page is actually a good habit for your kids to get into. In school they should put a date on every page they write on, as well as every handout they receive. Once they've titled and dated the first page they're ready to begin. Start by having them write down all the questions, so they can use this as a reference. There is no need to write down all the questions on each page everyday. After just a few repetitions they will have learned the questions by heart.

Have them title and date the next page, write the letter **W** on the left side of the page and answer the first question. After they have answered the first question have them right the letter **I** on the left side of the page, answer that question and continue with the other two questions.

By the way, I strongly suggest you do this as a family, everyone having their own book and doing the exercise. Whether you all do the exercise at the same time each day is up to you. I think it would be great to do it that way, but schedules being what they are, work out the timing as best you can.

What did you Win at yesterday?

Have them list everything they won at over the past twenty-four hours, everything that went well for them, everything they succeeded at, every person they helped, everything they did to make life a little better. This would include anything they did to contribute to their family, friends, school, community, religious organization, pets, plants, etc. You get the idea.

Sometimes people doing this for the first time will have difficulty finding things to put on the list. That's just fine; it will get easier with practice. In the beginning feel free to help your kids identify their wins. As time goes by we want them to identify their wins for themselves because what you might perceive as a win they might not and vice versa. Once they've completed their list they're ready to move onto the next question.

What Improvements could you make?

Now is the time to notice how they could have made things go better. Did they make any mistakes? If so, how could they correct them? If something went right, how might they have improved upon their performance? Have them look over their day and make their list.

A word here about learning from our mistakes. Yes, learning from our mistakes can be a very good thing. However, a few years ago I heard Tiger Woods say something very interesting about this. Tiger was being interviewed after a round of golf in which he did not play up to his standards. The journalist asked him if there was something he had learned today from his mistakes? Tiger looked at the journalist somewhat incredulously and told him he never pays attention to his mistakes. He focuses on what he did right and works to do those things even better. I found this to be a quite unique and wise point of view; something worthy of consideration.

What will your Next wins be?

Once they have finished listing their improvements they are ready to consider what they will be successful at over the next twenty-four hours. Have them list as many wins as they need to ensure a successful day. Sometimes all it takes is one significant win to make the day a rousing success. Sometimes it might take 10 or more. Most often somewhere between three and seven will do.

They should use their list of improvements to help them create their list of Next Wins. You should encourage them to mine various aspects of their lives for potential successes like they did earlier as they listed their wins for the previous day. Once again, this could include anything they can do to contribute to their own goals or those of their family, friends, school, or community.

If all this went well what State would you be in?

Finally, they need to consider what state they would be in, what attitude or outlook they would have if everything went their way. Once they have named that state, and optimally we are looking for a one or two word name, have them take a few minutes and imagine what it would be like to be in that state throughout the day.

There is an old Chinese saying, "As in the beginning, so in the end." In our society we are repeatedly taught that events and things bring us states of being. "If I get that car, I'll be so happy." "When I get that raise I'll be on top of the world!" "If she agrees to go out with me, it will make my day!" This is generally our experience of life. This is the effect position.

Remember, there is also a cause position. If we take on the attitude, occupy the state we believe we will experience if things go our way in the beginning, before we engage, the chances of us being successful and ending up with the attitude we expect as the result of success goes way, way up. So, if we begin as we hope we will end, our chances of ending up as we hope significantly increase.

By answering the question, *If all this went well what state would you be in?* and using their imagination to get them there at the beginning of the day, your son or daughter can greatly increase the likelihood the day will go their way.

As I said, WINS is an incredibly powerful tool. Could you imagine your children doing this every day for a month? How many wins do you think they would become aware of? How many successes over the course of the month do you think they might create? How much pride and self-satisfaction to you think they might experience? How many people do you think they might help? What do you think it would do to their attitude? Now imagine them doing this for a year . . . five years . . . a decade . . . a life time. What might it be possible for them to accomplish? What quality of life might they create for themselves?

Re-Minding™

The above are very simple, effective approaches that work to give you control of your attitudes. There are times, though, when they are not enough. Sometimes one needs a bigger crowbar. If these exercises do not work well enough for you or your children, there are other, more potent exercises that will. Re-Minding™ is a powerful set of tools that, through the use of strong imagery, allows you to literally reconstruct your mind. Re-Minding™ is the work of Dr. Samuels. It's easy to learn, fun to practice, and wondrously effective.

This is neither the time nor the place in which to explain these exercises and show you how they work, that would require an entire book. Fortunately, that book is being written. If you're interested, please visit www.drjimsamuels.com.

Predicting People and Choosing Partners

You can't eat your friends and have them too.
Budd Schulberg

Who our children hang out with is so, so important. Who they choose as friends can be the difference between trouble and the honor society. It is in choosing their peers that teaching our children about attitudes can be priceless. If your kids run with a pessimistic, unmotivated crowd the chances are they will become like those with whom they hang out. At the same time, if your kids are friends with optimistic, motivated young people who have clear plans for their futures, there's a great chance your kids will also.

While it is true that alligators marry alligators and that pessimistic people generally seek out other pessimistic people, children in their teens can often be very malleable. Some of our kids are leaders, some are not leaders yet. For those who are not yet leaders, hanging out with the right friends will put them at great advantage.

If our children learn to differentiate between people with dysfunctional and functional attitudes, and understand the importance of doing so, they will have a huge leg up. The bottom line is people with negative attitudes are rarely successful; somewhere along the way they're going to screw up. People with positive attitudes are almost always successful; they will find a way to make things work and help everybody win.

The best guarantee that your children will choose the right friends, friends who care and support one another, friends who are optimistic about themselves and their futures, friends who are loving and compassionate, is to ensure that your children are like the people with whom you wish them to associate. Teaching your children how to create attitudes that will best help them become such people is an essential step in their development.

Reputations: You'll never know why you didn't get the gig.

It's not what you know, it's who you know. I'm sure many of you have heard this aphorism. There is a second part to it . . . it's not only who you know, it's who knows you. More specifically it's what others know about you. More specifically still, it's what others believe they know about you. So, what do others believe they know about you? This, in essence is your reputation.

Your reputation may be the most important thing you have. A bad reputation will leave you little room to maneuver and will close many doors to you. A good reputation can give you lots of room and open doors in abundance. You've seen it in your school over and over. One student, having a reputation for turning in late assignments, turns an assignment in late with a very good and true excuse. Another student having a reputation as a diligent student also turns an assignment in late with a poor excuse. Who does the teacher give room to?

You all have reputations. When your name comes up people believe certain things about you, some of them false and some of them true. These beliefs are your reputation and they can stay attached to you for a long time. And your reputation may have impacts that you will never be aware of.

There is a teacher at your high school who, unbeknownst to you, will leave teaching two years after you graduate and go into finance. Ten years later you are applying for your dream job at some Wall Street brokerage firm. This job is amazing, the pay is great, the hours are sweet, and the firm will find you a great place to live in New York. It's perfect!

What you don't know is that the teacher who left your high school all those years ago is now responsible for hiring at that brokerage firm. As he's going through a stack of resumes your name rings a bell to him. With just a little research he confirms you were one of his students. Your career now is in his hands.

What does he remember about you? If he remembers you as a jerk, you will not get the job and you will never know why. If he remembers you quite fondly, you will certainly have a leg up on the other applicants . . . and if you land the job, you'll find out why. This is often the way things go in the world. Someone who has had some dealings with you tells someone else what she thinks about you and some result flows from there.

Some years ago there was a guy I had worked with who I did not think well of. In my estimation his approach to our work was unprofessional and inappropriate. A few years later he happened to be applying for a position in my good friend's business. My friend, reading his resume, realized this applicant and I may have worked together, so one evening as we were taking a walk my friend asked me about this gentleman. By the next morning my friend threw his resume in the trash. The applicant will never know.

Getting a reputation is relatively easy; changing a reputation can take months or years. Being young, it is easier for you to change your reputation because teachers and others in authority, for the most part, enjoy seeing young people do well. We expect them to make mistakes *and are encouraged when they fix them. Though reputations can be rehabilitated, your best move is to establish the reputation you want as early as possible.*

So what reputation do you have? What reputation do you want? The choice is yours.

Chapter Six

Creating the Future: Goal Setting,

Planning and Organization

"I learned this, at least, by my experiment: that if one advances con-fidently in the direction of his dreams, and endeavors to live the life which he had imagined, he will meet with a success unexpected in common hours."

Henry David Thoreau

The best way to predict the future is to create it . . . and the first step in creating the future is deciding what you want it to be. Many people leave the future up to chance. If your children are going to have the best chance to live the lives you wish for them, it will be to their great advantage to understand how goals work, become skilled at setting them, and know how to pursue them.

Yes, setting goals is a skill, a skill that is very often taken for granted. For some reason we seem to think it's part of the soft-ware that comes with our original operating system. We are no more born with the ability to set goals than we are with the ability to dribble a basketball, play the piano, or memorize information. Goal setting is a skill, and like any other, to do it effectively your children must learn how.

Once they are capable at setting goals, the next step towardscreating the future they want is to learn how to plan for their accomplishment. Once they can draw up workable plans, the next step is to learn how to manage the resources available to them, primarily money, space, and time.

Understanding Goal Setting

What's your goal? "I want to make money." "To be happy." "I'm going to lose weight." "To run a marathon." "To be healthier." All good goals, yes? Not really. Actually, only one of the above is a goal, do you know which one?

Goals Defined

Goals are endpoints that we are working to achieve. The more clearly defined and measurable the endpoint, the better the goal, and when I say 'better the goal' I mean the more likely it is to be accomplished.

Of the goal statements above only one refers to a clear end point . . . "To run a marathon." The others are not goals, they are purposes. Purposes and goals are different. Purposes are directions, goals are endpoints. 'Going east,' is a purpose, going to a particular city east of where you are, is a goal. To accomplish the purpose of going east all you have to do is take a single step towards the east and thus, your purpose is fulfilled. Accomplishing meaningful goals usually requires a little more.

You want to make money? Here's a dollar. You're done. You want to be healthier? Here's a carrot. If you eat it, you will be a little healthier. How much money do you intend to make? What can you do that will indicate you have achieved a measure of health that satisfies you? You get the idea.

This being said, purposes are senior to goals, they should come first. Optimally our goals flow from our purposes. Accomplishing a goal is more meaningful if it is linked to a higher purpose. The purpose answers the question, "Why?" "Why do you want to run a marathon?" "I want to run a marathon so I can challenge myself and prove to myself that I can get in shape." "Why do you want to get 3.5 GPA?" "I want to get a 3.5 so I can go to the college of my choice." "Why do you want to weigh 140 pounds?" "I want to weigh 140 pounds so I will feel better about myself." Your purpose is the answer.

There is another important aspect to consider when thinking about goals. A goal is an image that we are **working** toward accomplishing. This working aspect is critical. If a person is not working toward the accomplishment of their goal, what they are claiming is their goal actually is a want or a wish. In fact, if you want insight as to what a person's actual goals are, look at what they are, in fact, working on.

In 2001 a mother called me to help with her daughter, a senior in high school, who was concerned that she was not going to be able to get into her favorite college. When I met with them I asked the daughter what her goal was, and she told me her goal was to go to the University of Oregon. Great! I then asked her what she does. She told me about her job. She told me about the school choir. She told me about her boyfriend. She told me about how much she enjoyed dancing.

After she finished telling me about all these activities I looked at her and said, "Getting into the University of Oregon is not your goal, you're not doing anything to get there."

At this point her eyes bugged out and she looked at her mom and exclaimed, "Did he talk to dad?"

No, I hadn't spoken with her father. What he and I both knew though was that people act out their goals. Once again, if you want some insight into people, look at what they are doing.

How Goals Get Set

Goals are endpoints we are working to achieve. To be more specific, goals are images of endpoints in our mind that we are working to achieve. Purposes are more ambiguous images; they have no clear endpoint. It is important to put goals where they belong . . . in our mind. Goals are creatures of our mind. You cannot find a goal in the physical universe; the physical universe is simply a set of conditions. Keep this in mind. (No pun intended.)

Now, think about this: most of the goals we have, we did not set. They are not our goals. Let me repeat that. Most of the goals we are acting upon, we did not set. They are not our goals. They are the goals of our parents, our friends, advertising agencies, our society at large . . . and for the most part we are unaware of them.

Remember when you were a teenager hanging out with your friends watching television on a Saturday afternoon? Perhaps you just ate lunch an hour ago. As you were watching TV, a Pizza Hut ad came on, and 15 or 20 minutes later you and your friends decided pizza would be a good idea. Has that ever happened to you? If it has, the goal of getting pizza was activated, and it wasn't yours. It wasn't as if it was time for lunch and you and your friends were deciding what you were going to eat. You had seen this ad, or one like it, dozens or hundreds of times. This time the advertiser won.

As a graduate student at UCLA I was teaching a research methods class. I don't recall what prompted the question but at one point during a break I asked the 30 or so students, "Who here is planning to get married and have children?" Every student raised their hand immediately. Do you honestly believe that these 20 and 21-year-old young men and women had given that question the serious consideration that it requires, and by giving it that consideration making it a goal of their own? Being married and having children are two goals that just about every facet of our society promotes, and we have experienced those promotional efforts almost since we were born.

Most of us seem to assume that getting married and raising a family is automatic, and it is this kind of assumption that is a strong indicator that a goal is not truly our own. How many of us made such assumptions when deciding on our career path? This certainly, is not to say that there is anything wrong with getting married and having kids. Lord knows if people didn't do so, I wouldn't have as much to talk about. It is, however, to point out that people make such momentous decisions without ever considering whether marriage is right for them, and if marriage is right for them, is having children the best use of their time and energy?

Distinguishing between the goals we intentionally set and the other goals that are in our mind is important. Most people assume that goals are things they want. Sometimes this is true . . . and sometimes it's not. It's true when the goals we set are set intentionally. It is not necessarily true for the other goals that are set without our awareness. We might want some of these goals, if we thought about them. Some of these goals are innocuous. Some of these goals are not what we want at all. It's kind of stunning; we actually have goals in our mind we do not want.

So, how do goals get set in our mind? It all starts with attitude. Our attitudes determine what events and images our mind will be predisposed to noticing. Is your attitude one of rebellion? If so, your mind will be predisposed to events and pictures having to do with problems that bother or anger you. Is your attitude one of success? If so, your mind will be predisposed to noticing events and pictures having to do with solutions that make you feel happy and satisfied. As in so many arenas, attitude rules.

Goals as well as purposes, in large part being dependent upon our attitudes, get set through repetition and/or impact. If the thought/image is repeated often enough, our mind will accept it as a goal. If emotional content is added it will be accepted more quickly and more deeply. Think Pizza Hut commercial. It is the business of advertisers to repeatedly present us with images so much so that if the advertisers are successful those images will become our goals. And it is why sex is such a large component of the advertising we are exposed to. It's the advertiser's effort to add emotional content.

Since we were young children, our parents have told us lovingly that we're going to grow up, find someone we truly love, get married, and raise a family. Our parents tell us this with the best intentions in their hearts. One of their roles is to help guide our aspirations, so it is not surprising most of us have these goals.

Goals can also get set by impact. Sometimes we have such a painful experience that we spend our lives working to 'never do that again.' Sometimes an experience is so, so amazing that we try to recapture it for the rest of our lives. Either way, at times a single impact can set a goal.

What Our Mind Does With a Goal Once It Has One

Down through the centuries people have made many claims regarding what our minds are capable of. Fantastic powers have been attributed to them. People have asserted that the act of thinking by itself can bring about significant changes in the physical universe. Oh, were it only true.

Our minds are powerful, though not in the way some people think. They certainly play a large role in how we experience the universe. The actual power of the mind is nowhere more evident than in its activities while pursuing goals. During any given day there are an infinite amount of things we can pay attention to . . . if we had infinite attention. It is the role of our mind to bring to our attention those things that are related to the goals in it.

Imagine you are an elementary school teacher. Look around the room you're sitting in and from the viewpoint of an elementary school teacher make a few notes about the room. You might have noticed the size of the room, its safety features, the resources available to teach students, and the number of chairs available. Now, imagine you are an interior designer. From that viewpoint look around the room you're sitting in and make a few notes about the space. From this viewpoint you might have noticed the colors in the room, the ornamentation, and the lighting. Everyone I do this little thought experiment with comes up with two very different sets of notes. Within the construct of the exercise each viewpoint became a goal. What we see in our world is in large part determined by the goals in our mind.

This is what the mind does in its pursuit of goals. It brings information to us that it assesses to be relevant to the goal on which it is operating. This is quite a powerful function. Harkening back to our discussion of attitudes, this explains why it is so difficult for a pessimist to be successful and why success is so much more likely for the optimist. The goal the pessimist's mind is pursuing is the goal of failure. Of course this is not what the pessimist wants. It is however, what his mind is pursuing. So in a world of potential wins and losses, the pessimist's mind presents information about the potential losses. On the other hand, the mind of the optimist presents its owner with information relevant to success.

Goal Orientation

Purposes and goals are oriented in one of two ways: single positive or double negative. The difference between these two orientations is striking. Single-positively oriented purposes and goals are structured in a manner that reaches for something desirable to the individual. 'To raise healthy children,' 'To earn a Ph.D.,' 'To own a house,' are all examples of single positively oriented purposes and goals.

Double-negatively oriented purposes and goals are structured in a manner that retreats from something undesirable. 'To not be ill,' 'To lose 20 pounds,' 'To stop smoking,' 'To not be such a jerk,' are all of examples of double negatively oriented purposes and goals. Each has a condition that is considered undesirable or negative and is stated in such a way as to attempt to negate it.

This is not to be confused with assessing whether goals are positive or negative, good or bad. If a person believes that robbing a bank is desirable, then the goal to rob a bank is a single-positively oriented goal. Bank robbery is not a goal we would consider good, it's not a goal we would want people to accomplish, yet for the purposes of understanding goal orientation it is positively oriented.

Orientation matters to our minds. Remember, goals and purposes are images, and while it is fairly straightforward to create a picture of owning a house, complexity arises when we try to create a picture of not having something we don't want. It's like trying not to think of an elephant. Try it. Close your eyes and don't think of an elephant. What happened? Unless you altered the instruction in some way, it is almost impossible not to have a picture of an elephant come to mind.

Take the goal: 'To stop smoking. The first image we have to create in order to see ourselves stopping smoking is the image of us actually smoking. Then we have to see ourselves stopping. Unfortunately, our mind does not really see the 'stopping,' it sees the 'smoking;' just like the elephant. So, if we think about this a lot we present our mind with many images of smoking, often with some emotional content, and our mind accepts smoking as the goal. And once it accepts smoking as the goal, it goes about its business of bringing all manner of information regarding smoking to us. This makes it harder to fulfill our intention.

You see, minds are singularly unintelligent. It is for us to bring intelligence to them. In this regard our minds can be looked at as kind of like computers. Computers calculate and process information, they cannot decide the value of what they do. That is for us to do. The computer cannot decide if we will surf the web today or write that report that's due by Friday. This is our choice. We are the ones who bring intelligence to the computer's output. Similarly, we are the ones responsible for bringing intelligence to our mind. By using our intelligence we can have a large say in the programming of our mind, and one of the chief ways we do this is through setting goals.

Walk through a supermarket with someone trying to 'lose' weight. For most of us dieting is a significant aspect of weight loss and, for the most part, we conceive of diets as not eating fats or sweets. When you follow someone through a grocery store who's trying not to eat fats or sweets just notice what parts of the store they move most slowly through. Their mind is just doing its job.

People successfully stop smoking and successfully diet all the time. But there are many more people who are unsuccessful. A double-negative orientation doesn't make it impossible, it just makes it more difficult. We grasp single-positively oriented goals, instructions, and suggestions more easily. If you walk into a classroom and upon entering the teacher instructed you not to sit down, you would go through a certain process to figure out what's next; where does she want me stand; what does she want me to do? If that same teacher instructed you to line up against the wall, the process you would go through would be much simpler.

So, if you want to ensure that your son's mind is allied with his intentions, help him set single-positively oriented goals. If you notice that a goal he is working on is double-negatively oriented, have him change its orientation. Have him state his goal in such a way that its accomplishment precludes what it is he doesn't want. For example, if he wants to lose weight . . . what would he like to weigh? If he wants to stop procrastinating . . . he might set the goal, 'To have all his work done by 7:00 in the evening.' If he doesn't want to get another D in English . . . he might set the goal, 'To get a C or better on every test and assignment." With a little practice creating positively-oriented goal statements will become very easy.

Once he has his goal positively oriented the next step is to practice visualizing and experiencing what it is he wants. Have him see himself getting on that scale weighing 140 lbs and have imagine what it will feel like. Have him see himself completing all his work by 7:00 and relaxing knowing his work is done. Have him see himself getting A's and B's in English and have him feel the sense of pride that will come with such an accomplishment.

As you go through your day, notice how often you, your family, and others orient in a double-negative manner. You are doing it when you tell your kids 'Don't play in street.' 'Don't ruin your appetite,' 'Get off the computer.' 'Leave your brother alone.' Rather than telling your kids what you don't want them to do, you would be much better off telling your kids what you want them to do, 'Play in the yard.' 'If you're hungry, have a piece of fruit.' When you are helping your children set goals, teach them about orientation and help them develop orientations that are positive.

Teaching Your Children to Goal Set

> *You've got to be very careful if you don't know where you're going, because you might not get there.*
>
> Yogi Berra

"How do you want to be when you grow up?"

The best goals flow from our purposes. When we asked children that most ubiquitous of questions, "What do you want to be when you grow up?" we are asking them to explore goals. Kids get this question in a myriad of ways throughout their lives. As they get older they are asked to investigate the kind of careers they may be interested in. In high school they're asked what will their major be in college, in college they are asked again about careers. These are all good questions and worthy of exploration.

While kids are presented with numerous opportunities to explore their goals, they are presented with considerably fewer opportunities to explore their purposes. Exploring their purposes would make exploring their goals even more meaningful. Rather than, "What do you want to be when you grow up," you would do well to ask them to explore, **"How do you want to be when you grow up?"**

Answering this question requires exploring the qualities they want in their life, and this is so often overlooked. Optimally their choice of friends, partners, career paths can all be informed by this exploration. Encouraging your children to clearly determine the qualities of life that are important to them can help them choose people and paths that best suit them.

I've known so many people who have invested large sums of attention, energy, time, and money pursuing careers only to find out that those careers were not for them. I've known even more people who have gotten married only to discover that their idea and their spouse's idea of a good life were not compatible. I'm not sure why it is that we assume that quality-of-life will take care of itself. It is such a critical aspect, if not the most critical aspect of creating our futures.

You can start asking your children to consider quality when they are very young. It's as simple as asking five year old Melinda how she wants to go to the zoo. Does she want to go there happily? Does she want to be excited? Does she want to be interested? You can even ask young children how they want to be when they grow up. Their answers might surprise you. More importantly you'll be providing them with opportunities to consider the question.

As your children get older, this question will take on more meaning. When it was time for my nephew's bar mitzvah, his parents sat down with him to discuss what he wanted. All options were on the table. My brother and sister-in-law asked him what he valued most and, after some thought, my nephew decided upon family connection and fun. It was most important to him that our large, extended family had a good time together. My brother and his family proceeded accordingly, created a unique event, and a great time was had by all who attended.

As your children reach high school and college the question of **how** they want to be becomes increasingly essential as the effects of their decisions become more far reaching and encompassing. Consideration of quality can make all the difference.

Challenging, Rewarding, and Do-able

This is where skill and experience really come in. It takes practice for your kids to learn what they are actually capable of. One has to be pretty adept in order to set goals for themselves that are challenging and rewarding, as well as do-able. For a goal to be motivating it has to be challenging enough for it to make some demands on them, rewarding enough to make it worth their time and energy, and do-able enough for them to believe they have a realistic chance of accomplishing it.

It is not unusual for people to set goals for themselves that require too much or too little and so do not allow them to tap into their motivational energy. This happens with many New Year's resolutions. "I'm going to exercise four days a week this year." Really? How often did you exercise last year? If you exercised two or three days a week last year, this may be realistic. However, if you haven't exercised much in the last five years, you're most likely setting yourself up to miss your mark.

When your children accomplish a goal that's meaningful to them they should feel happy, they should have a sense of pride, and they should be excited. If they are not having these experiences, the goal they set didn't really matter. If we look around we'll see lots of people who we consider to be successful yet are not enjoying their lives. They are simply not accomplishing goals that matter enough to them.

Help your children by giving them opportunities to find their own meaning, and learn their own capacities. If they do set a goal that is too easy and complete it, talk with them about their feeling of accomplishment. If they are blasé, teach them. Either their goal did not matter to them or it was beneath their capacities. Then work with them to come up with a more motivating goal. If they take on a goal that is too much for them, please don't try to stop them . . . let them fail, then teach them. Have them come up with ways they could have set a better goal. Remember, they are learning a skill.

Arenas for Setting Goals

Encourage your children to set goals in a variety of arenas. Younger children can set goals for the health of their body, their family relationships, their relationships with their friends, their pets, their learning, and their art and music projects. As they get older they can include setting goals for developing their self-identities, for relating with girlfriends and boyfriends, for their participation in groups, for interacting with humanity as a whole, for their spiritual expression and their relationship with God or some infinite force.

I've likely left out some, but you get the point. For our children to become well-rounded individuals they should engage in a number of arenas in such a way that they develop balance.

Targeting

Once again, when you are teaching your children to set goals teach them to make their goals well defined. The more well-defined the target, the greater the chance they will be successful. There was a great scene in the movie, "The Patriot.," with Mel Gibson. For those of you who have not seen it, it takes place during the Revolutionary War. The British had just taken his character's older son and were marching him off to be interrogated and executed. To save his son he gets his two youngest sons to help him ambush his elder son's captors. When he's laying his trap he positions each of his young boys behind a fallen tree, gives each of them a gun, and says,

"Remember what I taught you?"

His sons, nervously looked back at him, "Yes dad. Aim small, miss small."

Aim small, miss small. What he taught them is if you aim for the bull's-eye and miss, you are likely to miss the bull's-eye entirely. If you aim for a tiny dot in the bull's-eye and miss, you still have a good chance to hit the bull's-eye. If your daughter's goal is specific enough and she comes up a little short, she is still likely to get close to it and still accomplish a lot. If she has a 2.9 GPA, sets her goal to have a 4.0, and winds up with a 3.8, is that a win or loss? Well, it's a little of both, and much more of a win.

The Measure of All Things

Paraphrasing the ancient Greek philosopher Protagoras, it is often said, "Man is the measure of all things." We absolutely are when it comes to goal setting, for it is we who will determine how our success is measured. For some goals such as those regarding grades, money, and foot speed, measurement is easy and obvious. For other goals in areas such as satisfaction, love, and justice, measurement is not as straightforward. It is here that goal setting often morphs to purpose fulfillment.

Behavioral psychologists might have you operationalize the concepts of satisfaction, love, justice. That is, they might have you decide upon a behavior that represents love, such as a hug, and have you count up how many you give and receive. This is one way to do it, though for some it may seem a bit artificial. If this seems too artificial for you, you can rate your outcomes on a 10 point scale. For example, if you have a purpose to have experience more ease in your life, you can simply rate your level of ease of on a scale of 0 to 10. It's subjective . . . and it works. It is your life, after all.

You may also leave pursuits of these types in the category of purposes and commit to goals that you believe would fulfill these purposes. I certainly have purposes to be happy and fulfilled. Rather than trying to specifically define these, I set goals which I believe will bring me happiness and fulfillment, for instance writing this book. The approaches you decide to teach your children just have to work well enough.

Failure and Success

One of the most fundamental judgments we tend to make is whether we have failed or succeeded. Did we win the race? Did we get an A? Have we been a good partner? Based upon our answers we often judge whether we are failures or successes; and we judge our children similarly. Of greater import, we teach our children to judge their own failures and successes. This can seem to make sense; however, it can be a very limited view. I would much rather children learn that the primary difference between a person who fails and a person who succeeds is where that person stops. A person oriented on success who does not meet her mark does not think, 'I didn't meet my mark.' A person oriented on success thinks, 'I didn't meet my mark **yet**.' Then she gets back to work.

Even better, a truly enlightened successful person simply arranges the game so they must win. This person sees the advantage, sees the win in every situation, and every outcome. Are there better outcomes than others? Of course. So what? Take your wins where you can get them and move on to greater ones.

Some years ago I learned of a CEO of an insurance company, I believe in Chicago who, upon receiving what was considered to be bad news, would respond by telling the bearer of the news, "That's great!" He truly believed there was advantage to be had in every event. Responding the way he did, focused his attention on searching for the advantages until he found them. Imagine the bewilderment of a new vice-president going to his boss with horrendous news for the first time and having his boss tell him, "That's great!" What must the V.P. have thought? "The old man's lost it," or some such assessment. I would certainly love to be fly on the wall of that office.

Teaching your children to find the advantage in every situation will help inoculate them against the vagaries of life. Stuff happens to all of us, none of us make it through unscathed. The way in which your children will weather the storms that buffet them in part determines how well they experience their lives. Teaching them to seek the advantage can ensure that they will experience their lives happily.

How well and how often your children accomplish what they set out to do are significant factors in determining the quality of life they experience. Teaching them how to explore their purposes, set positively-oriented goals, and assess their progress will certainly make their lives more, fun, exciting, and fulfilling.

Planning for Success

If few people have clear goals, even fewer have clear, workable plans. Go into any organization and ask, "What is your mission?" How many employees do you think will be able to answer accurately? If you dig a little deeper and ask for the organization's goals, what do you think you'll find? If an employee knows the mission and the goals do you think s/he will know the organization's plans? You can go all the way up the ladder to the vice presidents, to the president herself, and I bet there would not be but a handful of them that know the answers.

Now, every company I've worked and consulted for has had a mission statement. Heck, I helped to create some of them. The company's management team went on a weekend retreat to develop one. They also all have goals. They've had consultants come in and help develop them. I have been one of those consultants. Many even have plans for their goals' accomplishment. So what gives? It has been my experience that mission statements, goals, and plans wind up in someone's drawer or in some file on someone's computer never to be looked at again.

But this is not the way it is everywhere. Some years ago I was visiting my cousin in Colorado and he took me to his place of business. He is an optical engineer working for Ball Aerospace and Technologies, one of the engineering concerns at the top of the aerospace food chain. My cousin was part of the team that designed the mirror that replaced the original, faulty one on the Hubble Telescope. At the time of my visit he was working on a research satellite, "Deep Impact," whose mission it was to explore comets. By the way, I understand it did so with much success in 2007.

As he was taking me around the facility and showing me the spacecraft (unfortunately . . . and wisely, he wouldn't let me get my hands on it) I saw, along a 15 to 20 foot wall of the main workspace, the plans. The plans were a color coded time-line specifying what needed to be done, when it needed to be done by, and who was responsible for each step. It struck me that this was the first time I had seen a project's plans, any project's plans, up in a place for all to see. Talk about being on the same page! I thought back to all the organizations for whom I had worked and consulted.

Having a clear goal sets the target. Having clear, workable plans lays down the path. Without a good plan, many endeavors are destined to fail. I have asked thousands of students if they have goals. About 85% do, and proudly tell me. When I ask them how they will accomplish their goal, I almost always get blank faces. They don't know. Maybe 20% give me some generalized response. Of the 20% who have some idea, only about a quarter of them tell me in more specific terms. If I push further and ask if they have a written plan, I get nothing.

How do we expect them to be successful? It seems we spend a fair amount of time encouraging our kids to come up with goals. Not so much when it comes to helping our kids come up with plans for their accomplishment. One of the results of our kids not learning to develop plans is they come to believe goals are not really connected to the physical universe. This leads to the grave error of leaving out the 'working towards its accomplishment' component of the goal. Many of our kids are walking around thinking they have goals, not understanding they have nothing of the sort. If they do not connect their goals to the physical universe, through some kind of meaningful plan their 'goals' are no more than wishes.

Even when they do have plans, if they are not acting on them, they do not have a goal. More accurately, the plans they are not acting upon do not reflect the goals they actually have. Only when they are doing things to accomplish the goals they set for themselves can we say the goal is genuinely real. So if you're going to help your children develop plans, do your best to make sure they are planning for their true goals. I guarantee planning with your children will be a lot more fun.

There are many reasons plans are so important. First and foremost they enable us to see where we're going. They are the map that gets us from here to there. Plans also serve a motivational purpose. When our goals are significant and their accomplishments are far in the future, each step of our plan provides us with smaller goals, the accomplishing of which enable us to keep our motivation high. So if you would like to teach your kids how to plan effectively here is an exercise to insure all the basics are covered.

PLANS (Samuels)
　　P: Purpose and Goal
　　L: Logic

A: Action Analysis

N: Numbered Steps

S: Schedule

Simply put, for a plan to be workable it must have a clearly defined purpose and goal, a logic for its accomplishment, an analysis of the necessary actions that demonstrate the plan is worth doing, and numbered action steps, each of which are scheduled with appropriate target dates. Oh yes, one more thing: for a plan to be useful, it has to be written down. As we have already addressed purposes and goals, let's move right to Logic.

Logic

How are you going to go about accomplishing your goal? Does this make sense? If you follow this path will you likely get there? Do you need to be more specific? Your logic will give you insight into how well you understand what it is you want to do. The more simple, straightforward, and complete your logic is, the more fully you understand the task ahead of you.

I was working with a ninth grader whose goal was to get a scholarship to play basketball at North Carolina. When I asked him how he planned to do it, he told me he was going to get good grades in high school and get a scholarship. Now I knew him in middle school and he was not particularly academically successful, nor was he an exceptional basketball player. When I asked him what he was going to do to make sure his grades were good enough and his basketball skills were superior, he didn't have much of an answer. His logic wasn't up to the task.

Take all the time you need to help your son or daughter work out the logic of pursuing their goal. As they get older and they understand how this works, encourage them to do it themselves. They will likely make mistakes. When they do make mistakes help them figure out how they can improve in the next round. Once again, this is all good; it's how we learn.

Action Analysis

Have you ever taken on a project that you came to learn was a mistake for you? You know, it was such a good idea, it was so exciting, doing it was a no-brainer. You didn't think too much about the cost or the amount of time it would take, it was not that hard and it was so, so worthwhile. Then you got into the project and realized it was going to cost four times as much as you thought and going to take three times as long. Halfway through you looked in the mirror and asked yourself, "What in God's name was I thinking?"

This has happened to everyone I know at least once. Some of us are bit more hardheaded than others and experience this with some frequency. It's one thing when we do this in our home, spend a couple hundred or couple thousand more dollars than we expected, and ruin four weekends. It's another thing when corporations do it, lose millions of dollars and are forced to lay off hundreds of workers. It's still another when our government does it, costing us billions of dollars. At every level this is the result of poor, little, or no consideration for the expense of a project.

Action analysis is that stage of planning where you consider, as accurately as you can, the costs associated with pursuing your project. Only after you have a reasonable estimate of these costs can you make a decision whether or not the project is worth it. In this stage of planning, applying your Logic, you create a list of all the steps you need to take to accomplish your goal, then for each step you figure out how much it will cost and how much time it will take to complete. This is called the ACT formula. **A**ctions. **C**osts. **T**ime. (Samuels)

When helping your son plan out some school project have him make a sheet with three columns:

Actions   Cost   Time

Have him list the steps and fill in the other two columns. If this is a school project he will likely not be making a judgment as to whether to do the assignment or not. School or not, your sons and daughters should do this whenever they are planning or exploring any goal.

Humans are notorious for underestimating the resources needed for projects, especially when it's a project we really want to do. So, when they are evaluating their actions in an arena that is relatively new to them it's a good idea to have them multiply the costs and time by a factor of three as projects have a tendency to require three times the money and time than we originally allot. As they get more experience in an area they can reduce this to a factor of two.

When they are finished not only will they have a better idea of how much their endeavor will cost and how much time it will take, they will also be able to evaluate if there is something better they can do with that money and time.

Numbering the Steps

Assuming the action analysis turned out favorably, that is they've decided it is worth it to pursue this goal, the next phase of planning requires that they put all the steps in order and number them. This gives them another chance to make sure everything is there and in its proper place.

Scheduling

The final phase in planning is fantastically important and often overlooked when people take the time to plan at all. Scheduling each step of your plan is how your plan interfaces with the physical universe. Time management specialists understand that if something isn't scheduled, and they mean recorded in some kind of planner, the probability of it getting done goes way down. If you write your tasks down or record them in some way, the chances of them being accomplished go up significantly. Of course this implies that your kids will have some sort of scheduling device. We'll address that in the next section.

One more thing: In addition to having their plans in a file on their computer or in a journal book . . .

Have them put their goals and plans in clear sight!

There you have it. This is what's necessary to create workable plans. The abilities to set goals and plan are essential for your children to thrive in the world today. When most people in the world, for all intents and purposes, are leaving their lives to chance, those who are willing and able to direct their lives are the ones who will be able to have the most success and do the most good.

Organization: From Chaos Comes Order

"My daughter's room is a mess; she can't even see the floor." "My son's school bag is so stuffed with papers, it's no wonder he loses his homework half the time." Sound familiar? The number one concern parents come to me with is motivation. Organizational issues follow close behind.

We are all familiar with the prime organizational principle, a place for everything and everything in its place. This prime principle has a slightly lesser known sibling, a time for everything and everything in its time. Following these principles quiets chaos and brings order.

Before we explore ways to help your children bring more order to their lives, two caveats. First, if your workspace appears disorganized to the outside world, you will likely have a steeper hill to climb helping your kids be more organized. Time and again I work with parents whose home workspace looks like a mess and who, at the same time, want their kid's desk and their kid's room to be a paragon of order. Very often kids learn their work habits from their parents.

Which brings me to the second caveat, the belief that the more orderly one's workspace is the better one will work; it is just that, a belief. I have seen too many brilliant, successful individuals whose workspaces look like a tornado just passed through. Personally, I'm one of the neat and orderly ones. As I sit here writing, other than my computer, there are two pieces of paper on my desk, both of which I need.

In 1986 when I arrived at UCLA to begin my graduate education I met with my advisor to discuss my first year's work. Allen Parducci was the best advisor imaginable, a true scholar who had the wisdom to understand the value, as well as the limits, of research. I will never be able to thank him enough for his guidance and friendship during my graduate years.

During our discussion he informed me that he would be traveling to France for nine months and offered me the use of his office. Well, for a graduate student to have a large office with windows looking out over the campus is a wonderful thing. Unfortunately for me, Dr. Parducci was one of those brilliant people who kept stacks of papers everywhere. There was not a clear surface in his room. While he, obviously, was able to work well in a space that for my tastes seemed quite chaotic, I knew I could not. I graciously thanked him and proceeded to clear out one of the rooms he used for his research in the basement and made that my office for the next 3 1/2 years.

Though I am a firm believer in the value of neat and orderly spaces, I remain sensitive to the likelihood that a few individuals can perform better in less organized environments. Your child might be one of these individuals. If they claim they are, make them prove it; and for my money the only proof is in the quality of their grades. If they are straight A students or close, let them work anywhere they want, anyway they want. For all others . . .

Managing Space

There is great value to being organized. Our physical space is often a reflection of our mental space. The more clarity we experience in our minds, the more orderly our physical space tends to be. This also works in the other direction. When we are bothered about something or feeling a little overwhelmed, cleaning our house or straightening out our office will help us feel better and quiet our minds.

When our children are on top of their game and feeling good, they tend to be a little more organized than usual . . . and vice versa. Teaching and encouraging them to manage their space well will help them on their road to success. Our kids have two spaces they need to have control of: the place where they do their schoolwork and their personal space in general.

Let's start with their personal space. If they have their own room, then that is the space they are responsible for controlling. If they share a room with their siblings, then it's their responsibility to control their part of the room.

If their room is a mess and they do not seem to be able to keep it tidy, most parents try one of two approaches: brute force or shut the door. The brute force approach involves some form of making your kids clean their room, often connected to some reward/punishment structure. Parents often take the shut the door approach when they tire of the brute force routine. Both of these approaches work to a degree. If, however, the former isn't working and the latter is not acceptable, you may want to try a third approach.

Think of it as the elephant eating approach. How do you eat an elephant? . . . One bite at a time. How does a child organize his space? One item at a time. Have your son select one thing that he wears or uses everyday, like his sneakers or book bag for school. Have him decide where he would like to keep this item. For the next three weeks have him keep his sneakers where he decided to keep them. Why three weeks? Because it takes about three weeks of doing something daily to establish it as a habit.

Feel free to attach whatever rewards you wish to this task. When he has been successful, do it again; only this time take two items for him to get under his control. Keep doing this until he has gained the ability to control his things.

There are some children who seem to be incapable of keeping their room together. Perhaps the habit of being unkempt has become deeply ingrained. Perhaps their organizational wiring has not taken hold yet. Whatever the reason, you may want to try this incremental approach. Slow and steady often wins the race.

Let's move on to the space which they use to do their school work. Where do your children do their schoolwork? Do they do it at the kitchen table? Do they have a desk in their room? Do they work in the family study? Wherever they work, their tools should be handy. They should have their school books and binder, writing implements, a dictionary and thesaurus, anything they use on a daily basis. If there is a family computer, that should be nearby; if they have their own computer, it should be at hand.

When your children are young teach them to prepare their workspace. Teach them to think about what they will need and then to make sure those things readily available. When they finish their work teach them to put everything back where it belongs. I am sure this is all pretty obvious, but I thought I'd mention it just in case.

Handling Papers: The Filing System

As our children get older they are going to need a filing system for all their school papers. One of the reasons students stuff papers in their binders and book bags willy-nilly is simply because they have no other place to put them that is easy for them to access. There are many ways they can organize their papers and many tools on the market to help them. Here is one basic approach.

First, they should have a file box or cabinet with file folders. This box can be a single drawer in a file cabinet, a stand-alone single drawer file cabinet, a cardboard file box; any of these will do just fine. I have also seen students use accordion folders with great effect. In this one box they should keep all their work organized in folders. They should have three folders for every subject or class they are taking. One folder should be for handouts, one should be for homework and projects they have already turned in, and one for homework and projects they have yet to turn in. When they get home from school each day they should take all the papers that they received and put them in their proper folder.

There is one more folder they need to add to make this system complete. It is this folder that holds the entire system together. The title of this folder should be, "Papers to Be Filed." It should be placed in the front of the file box or cabinet. It should be the first folder they see, and the easiest to access. If they are not sure where something should be filed or if they're simply not into filing today, this is the file their papers go in. Once a week they can take their time, go through this file, and put the papers in it where they belong. This allows them to always have a place for every paper. If they get into this habit they will always know where to find anything they need.

Time Management

The parents who come to me asking me to help their children manage their time most often tell me their kids are doing so much that they're having trouble keeping track of it all. After looking at their kid's schedule I sometimes suggest one way they can help them manage their time more efficiently is to give them more space in their weekly schedule. Perhaps they don't need to do all the things they're doing; perhaps a little breathing room might be just the thing for them. We all know how it is when we are handling as much as we can, and handling everything well by the way, and then taking on one more thing. Almost immediately we find we're not handling anything near as well as we were before. Children are no different.

Regardless of how much your children are doing, developing their ability to manage their time is important. There are a plethora of tools available to help them, from the daily planners that most schools give them, to the more business-like planners that you can find in any office supply store. I have been in homes and seen monthly calendars attached to refrigerators and larger ones blown up and put on the wall. Of course, getting your kids to use any of these can be a challenge.

If your child finds using these kinds of planners too cumbersome or complex, they might be more apt to use the electronic ones that come loaded on their cell phones or the more elaborate systems that are on their computers. Sometimes kids are reluctant to use the tools available to manage their time simply because they have no need for them. They already have management people in place . . . their parents.

This past summer my friend's 15-year-old daughter and 17-year-old son left home to work. His daughter got a job as a nanny for a family in New England and his son found work in London. Both did exceptionally well and had great summers. Both were very responsible and self-motivated, they got up early every morning and were on time every day, they worked diligently, and went the extra mile. They both received much praise from those they worked for. You could imagine my friend's surprise when at the beginning of the Fall school term neither of them would get themselves up to go to school. He has since resumed his duties as alarm clock.

Parents have been making sure their kids' assignments are done, their bags are packed, they know about soccer practice, they have their violin in tow, and so on since they started school. Parents have been the ones that told them when to do their homework, when to practice their instrument, when to get ready for school and the time of their basketball game. Can parents be too surprised when their sons and daughters get to high school and cannot manage their own time?

Remember, one of your roles as parents is to model the universe your kids will ultimately have to live in. The earlier you begin to transfer responsibility for managing their own time to your children, the sooner they will develop the skill. This means your children need to experience the consequences of managing their time poorly as well as managing their time well.

The first few times your son in junior high school doesn't get to go out with his friends because he was spending time gaming rather than spending that time doing his homework, will likely encourage him to learn to manage his time a little better. One day your daughter, a seventh grader, will leave a project until the last minute and expect you to drop what you're doing to help her, as you have done in the past. She will learn a lot about time management the first time you refuse to help and let her experience the consequences of not getting her assignment in on time.

It is up to you to help them see how managing their time well will lead to better outcomes. Every seven-year-old I know is capable of getting ready for school the night before. Every 12-year-old I know is capable of getting her homework done before going out on a Friday night. Every 15-year-old I know is capable of balancing his schoolwork, baseball practice, and hanging out with friends. Managing time is mostly a matter of learning how to do it and being motivated enough to apply what we've learned.

Understanding Money

Money is better than poverty, if only for financial reasons.
Woody Allen

If we are to do all that we can to guarantee our children's futures we must teach them about money. We must teach them about earning money. We must teach them about saving money and the power of compound interest. We must teach them about spending money and the cost of credit. Once again, I must say that money is not the measure of all things, far from it. However, it is a resource to be used to fulfill our purposes and accomplish our goals, and to this end we, as well as our children, should understand it.

Earning Money

We earn money by providing value. The more society values what a person does and the fewer people there are who can do it, the more money that person will earn. Berry Gordy, the founder of Motown, was once discussing the value of musical talent with a journalist. He told the journalist, and here I am paraphrasing:

"Musical talent is all around. I could go into any town in America, throw a rock and hit a dozen people who could sing, dance, or play an instrument well. There are many fewer people however, who can write a hit song, and there are only a small handful of people who could turn those singers and writers into stars. I'm one of the few."

I have hung out on the borders of the music world and from this vantage point I have been introduced to dozens of monster musicians. I suspect there are thousands of them, maybe tens of thousands. The vast majority of these musicians make little or no money from their talent. A few have broke into the industry and play professionally. While they can earn a good living, what they earn is a pittance compared to what successful songwriters earn.

And what these songwriters earn is a drop in the bucket compared to what impresarios like Berry Gordy earn.

According to the last census, about 25% of Americans over the age of 25 hold four-year college degrees, and approximately 3% of Americans over the age of 25 hold the title of Doctor in all its forms. Because our society puts a greater value on dentists than doctors of French literature, dentists tend to make more money . . . though it wouldn't surprise me if doctors of French literature are happier. This is why education is one of the more accepted paths to increased earning potential.

There is a myth believed by many that hard work produces money. Yes, hard work does produce money, but not necessarily a lot of it. People who work in meatpacking plants work extremely hard, yet they don't make much money. Smart work will produce more money than hard work almost every time.

We want to teach our children to work smarter. If they can come up with a method to get their schoolwork done correctly in less time, they should be encouraged. In this world we get paid when we do things right. We don't get paid nearly as much when we do things wrong . . . and if we do enough things wrong we don't get paid all. We tend to get paid the most when we get it right . . . fast.

Income is all about creating value as the society measures it. The question for our children is, 'How can they be valuable?' 'What value can they create?' Of course, it is incumbent upon us to teach our children that money is simply a means to an end and that the ends we pursue are truly the measure of who and what we are.

Saving Money and the Power of Compound Interest

I believe it was Albert Einstein who said, "Compound interest was man's greatest invention." The power of compound interest is the factor most responsible for wealth generation in our society. Investing $10,000 in a fund that grows at an interest rate of 7% a year will become well over $1 million in about 50 years. And that assumes you will not add any additional money to that fund over time.

Though, to paraphrase Leonard 'Bones' McCoy, "I'm not that kind of doctor." I do know that teaching our kids to save money, then helping them learn to invest wisely can make a huge difference in their lives. Most people who teach personal finance management suggest that the average person should put 10% of their earnings in some kind of savings account or into some kind of investment. I, of course, will not make any suggestions as to where one might put their money. I will just suggest that you teach your kids how much money can grow if invested properly, encourage them to save, and help them learn about investing.

Spending Money and the Cost of Credit

It is critical that our children learn the true cost of spending money and credit. I am stunned at how few teenagers seem to understand opportunity costs, and that fewer still understand how credit works. Rarely do they consider better uses for the money they are about to spend on that shirt they just must have; nor do they understand how much those clothes they bought on credit will actually cost them.

If they are to become fiscally savvy we need to teach them to ask themselves when they are shopping, "Can I put what I'm about to spend to better use?" As they get older they need to be able to compare the value of the $50 they are about to spend on a shirt with the value of investing that money. What can the $50 be worth in ten years? Could they put that $50 towards buying something they could turn around and sell for a profit? It can come down to, would they rather be wealthy later or look good now?

Which brings us to credit. Our kids have to learn how credit and the banks work. We have to show them the true cost of something bought on credit if it is paid off slowly. We have to teach them the difference between a credit card with a 12% interest rate and a credit card with an 18% interest rate and a credit card with a 24% interest rate. We have to help them understand the effects of missing a payment. They have to know that not only can banks charge them a $40 fee, they can also raise their interest rate up to 30% or more. And, by all means they have to understand their credit score, how it effects not only their ability to buy a car, but also to get a job. They also must know how to make sure their credit report is accurate

Our kids need to understand what the impacts will be on them for borrowing money to go to college. They need to understand how long it will take them to pay back their loans and how much money it will cost them per month to do so. They need to understand how much easier it is to work diligently for three years in high school to earn scholarships and grants than to borrow money for college and have to pay it back over twenty years.

Having these kinds of rudimentary understandings about money will go a long way toward preparing them to engage in the real world successfully. Far too many young people get into financial trouble early in their lives, trouble that could easily have been avoided with a little information. Our brief discussion here is only the very tip of the iceberg; there certainly is much, much more for them to know. My wish is that by the time they are ready to leave the home or go off to college they have a general understanding as to how to protect themselves and use our monetary system to their advantage.

How Good Teachers Go Bad

How many of you have had a bad teacher or two? Teachers that were boring, teachers that didn't like their students, teachers that simply didn't seem to care? I know I certainly have had my share. I bet a few of you even think most of your teachers aren't any good. Did you ever stop and wonder why? Didn't your school district know about them before they hired them? Actually, most teachers started out pretty good and some are even a lot better than that. All of them cared, all of them loved kids. They all loved their subjects. That's why they became teachers

So what happened to them? Glad you asked. Let me tell you how some teachers morph from caring, enthusiastic people to some of the teachers you do not like today.

For most teachers, their desire to teach began in high school or college. Somewhere along the way they likely had a truly inspiring teacher themselves. This teacher may have gotten them really excited about a subject or helped them see the world in a better way. They may have been so fortunate as to even have two, three, four, or more such teachers. So they decided to be one. Motivated by the urge to excite young people and help them transform, they began their teacher education.

After four of five years they finished their schooling and were ready to enter their first classroom. Now it's the first day at their first job. They are both excited and nervous. Will they be able to get to their students? Will they be able to manage their classroom? Will they be able to inspire? Will they be able to motivate their students to learn? These and dozens of questions like them are rattling around their brains.

The first day goes well enough; everyone is eager and getting introduced to one another. Being the first day, little work is supposed to get done. But now comes the second day when the real work begins. Our young teacher has prepared her lesson for the day. She has been working on her plans all summer and she believes they are exciting. The students walk into class, take their seats, and she begins.

As the period progresses she notices five students at the front of the room paying close attention. She notices two boys at the back of the room with their heads on their desks. She notices a couple of girls passing notes to each other, five other students texting, three students staring out the window, two other students laughing at some private joke, and nine others spaced out with blank, bored faces.

She asks a question out of her lesson plan and a student raises his hand. She enthusiastically calls on him expecting him to have something of value to contribute to the class. Instead of insight he asks her if he can go to the bathroom. After four other classes go more or less similarly she goes home believing that she has to change her approach. So she stays up most of the night revamping her lessons for the next day.

The next day goes a little better and she's encouraged, but the day after goes no better. She chalks all this up to her inexperience and is still committed to being a great teacher. Throughout the year she works and reworks her lessons, she talks with other teachers, she *calls her mentors at the schools she attended. She vows that she will be better next year.*

The next year comes and the year after that . . . and little changes. Try as she might she cannot interest any but a few students in each of her classes. After a few years it dawns on her, her students truly don't care. Oh, some of them care for grades but only a handful actually cares about learning. She finally gets it, it really doesn't matter what she does. The kids that come into her classroom would certainly rather be somewhere else . . . and given the option, would be gone in a heartbeat.

Teaching became just a job to her. She covers the material she is supposed to cover. Whether the students understand the material is not so important. She no longer creates new lesson plans, she has four years worth of them, and after all one lesson is as good as the next. Every year there are a few students who are interested and who she enjoys helping. As for the rest, they really don't matter much.

This is what happens to many of your teachers. At some point they tire of banging their heads against the wall of their students' apathy, so they do what's required of them and little more.

In every arena there are exceptional performers and teaching is no different. You have all had teachers that were exciting, brilliant, fun, and inspirational. Every school has a number of them. These are the rock stars, these are the amazing teachers. Also, in every arena the majority of the performers are average, solid performers who can do the job. Under the right conditions these average performers can become exceptional.

In the arena of education, just as a great teacher can elevate their students, great students can elevate the average teacher to the league of the exceptional teacher. How? You see learning is an exchange. For true learning to happen it requires both teachers and students to be engaged. It is for the teacher to bring their knowledge, wisdom, and enthusiasm. It is for the student to bring their enthusiasm, interest, and thirst to learn.

You and your peers have more power than you know. The more interest you bring into class, the more inspired your teachers will become which in turn will make them more exciting. When this occurs school becomes an amazing place to be. You and your peers can make it so, if you choose.

Chapter Seven

Putting It All Together: Evaluating, Adapting, Persisting, and Advocating

The ultimate measure of a man is not where he stands in moments of comfort and convenience, but where he stands at times of challenge and controversy.

Martin Luther King, Jr.

Evaluating

No battle plan survives first contact with the enemy. The clearest goal, supported by the most comprehensive plan will rarely, if ever, unfold the way originally intended . . . even if it is being administered by the most able of individuals. In addition to all the skills outlined in the previous pages, if your children are to bring their goals to fruition they must be capable of evaluating the world around them; adapting their purposes, goals, and plans accordingly; sticking with their plans until they are successful; and speaking up for themselves.

Being Interested in the World

Our world is changing rapidly and with all this activity comes increased complexity. Many people seem to be having a hard time keeping up. The major concerns that our children will have to address cannot be resolved into black and white. The environment, healthcare, our economy, foreign relations, war, and international government, are only some of the issues that will confront our children's generation . . . and all of these require nuanced understandings in order for them to chart the best path.

It is your responsibility to encourage your children to take an interest in the world and to prepare them as best you can to think through the many gray areas that they will encounter. You can start, if you haven't already, by taking an increased interest in the world yourself, then by having your kids do the same. You can develop the tradition as a family of watching the news, reading blogs, and/or surfing the web for interesting information pertaining to some current event, then having family discussions. It is important that you get your news and information from a variety of sources that hold a variety of viewpoints.

Showing your children that you value their views, respect their right to dissent, and welcome their arguments can lead to the most interesting and enlightening discussions which can broaden everyone's understanding. Discussions such as these can also teach your children how to listen to others' viewpoints, evaluate different positions, and agree and disagree constructively.

With a strong interest in, and understanding of, the world your children will be better able to see what lies ahead of them and so choose paths that offer them, their families, and their communities at large the best chance for health and happiness.

Critical Thinking

> *I think we consider too much the good luck of the early bird and not enough the bad luck of the early worm.*

Theodore Roosevelt

Along with taking an interest in the world, children of all ages should be encouraged to evaluate information and think for themselves. With the World Wide Web came an explosion of information. There can be no doubt we are in the information age. Just about anything we want to know we can find out with the click of a mouse or the brush of a finger. Neat deal, eh?

Yes and no. There is so much incomplete information, misinformation, and out and out false information mixed in with the good stuff that it is often difficult to sort out fiction from fact, lies from truth. Given that it is in the very nature of the technology to encourage the transfer of as much information as possible, it becomes the user's responsibility to do the sorting.

If your kids are going to grow up being more than yes men and women for pundits, advertisers, politicians and all manner of disingenuous entertainers, they will need to become adept at evaluating what they see, read, and hear. A skill you can teach to ready them for this task is to find out who is behind the information they are receiving and what is their likely purpose. Simply put, who is selling what to whom? When they see an ad, political or otherwise, on TV or Youtube, they should look to see who sponsored that ad. The sponsor's name is always somewhere in the picture. Once they have that name they should google it and check out their website. Once on their website, they can search around and find out who else the organization is affiliated with. In this way they can get a much better idea who really is selling what.

When they are doing research they need to develop the habit of checking for corroborating sources. Do your kids understand the limits of Wikipedia? Now, more than ever, it is crucial that your kids learn that reading something doesn't make it true; nor does hearing it or seeing it.

In the winter of 2009 I received an e-mail from a friend excited about an article he read with a proposal for solving our country's economic problems. He had passed it on to me. My friend is a bright, thoughtful man whose opinions I value greatly. The author proposed retiring everyone over the age of 50 and paying them each $1 million in return. The author argued that given there were 40 million workers over the age of 50 this would open up 40 million jobs and more than solve the unemployment problem. Furthermore those people receiving $1 million would pay off their mortgages and thus in part solve our housing problems. Finally, those people would spend the money on cars and the like bolstering the economy in general. To top it all off, all this would cost less than the economic bailout our government was proposing. Fantastic! Everybody wins!

What would you do upon receiving this e-mail? My friend, like tens of thousands of others, passed it on to his friends. I did the math and it was pretty simple. The economic bailout our government was proposing at the time would cost between two and four trillion dollars. I quickly multiplied 40 million people by $1 million and found out that the author's plan would cost $40 trillion, ten to twenty times the cost of the bailout. Before we could even consider whether the plan had merit, just the numbers alone made it silly. This is just one example of how misinformation gets passed around the world.

We have to encourage our children to wonder, question, and approach proposals and ideas with a healthy skepticism. By healthy skepticism I mean looking to see if the facts are accurate, if the logic holds up, if the numbers are real. This is quite different from skepticism that is not healthy in which the skeptic looks for evidence something is wrong,. A healthy skeptic looks to make sure a good idea can be made to work.

Attaining information has never been easier. Now we must develop the wisdom to understand and apply it. The ability to think critically, to think analytically, is crucial if we and our children are to engage in the world intelligently, and have a chance to solve our world's problems and create a society that provides all people fair and honest opportunities to thrive.

Adapting

In the last chapter, during the discussion of planning, I suggested it might be a good idea for your kids to multiply the time and money they estimated for a project by a factor of three. This will provide them a more accurate estimate of the actual cost of the project under consideration. This also reflects the great likelihood that they will have to adapt their plans to meet new realities.

Accepting the World as It Is

If our children are going to adapt successfully, they first need to learn to accept the world as it actually is. Accepting the world as it is does not mean they have to give up their goals. Accepting the world as it is does not mean they have to be a victim. Accepting the world as it is does not mean that they cannot change it. Accepting the world as it is simply means noticing what is in fact going on and adapting to give themselves the best chance of success.

Sometimes circumstances change and their plan has to change to be aligned with the new conditions. For example, their plan was to take the SAT twice, which they did. Unfortunately, neither time were their scores satisfactory. Change of plan. Now the plan is to take an SAT preparation class and take the SAT a third time.

Sometimes circumstances change so the goal has to change to be aligned with the new conditions. "Warning! Warning! Danger Will Robinson!" "Failure imminent!!" I hear some of you screaming. "After all, isn't changing your goal just a politically correct way to say failure?" Not when you have a purpose you wish to express. If your son's or daughter's goal flowed from a clear purpose, s/he could go back to that purpose and find another goal that would fulfill it just as well . . . maybe even better.

The goal was to go skiing, the weather did not cooperate, and your son is bummed. If you ask him why he wanted to go skiing, he might tell you he wanted to get out and have fun with his friends. Well, he and his friends are certainly able to find another way to have fun together. He might have said he wanted to go skiing because he loves it so much. If you ask him what it is about skiing that he so loves, you may be able to help him find another way for him to get the experience he desires. By digging a little deeper you can often get to the purpose he wants to express or the experience he is looking to have.

In 1985 I decided to apply to graduate school for my Ph.D. in clinical psychology. My grades in college were excellent; my overall GPA at Portland State University was a 3.79. Of the classes I took in my major area, psychology, I received one B and about twenty-two A's. On my GRE test (SAT's for graduate school) I averaged scoring in the top 6 percent in the nation and my recommendations were stellar. I was pretty cocky. I applied to the best programs on the West Coast and one program, Yale, on the east coast. At the time I thought I would only travel east for the very, very best.

My advisor at Portland State, Dr. Barry Anderson, a wonderful teacher and mentor, was certain I would be accepted into every program for which I made application. Thinking that was too optimistic, I bet him a glass of wine that I would be rejected by one school. To both his and my and amazement I was rejected by them all.

What was I to do? I still wanted to go to graduate school. Time to change plans. I thought to myself, 'It's not what you know it's who you know, so I better get to know some people.' I proceeded to get a list of professors at each school in which I was interested, chose one from each whose work excited me, studied their work, and then went to meet them. I met professors at Stanford, Berkeley, and the University of Oregon.

I had also wanted to meet a professor at UCLA, Dr. Gerry Goodman. Unfortunately I didn't have the opportunity to get in touch with him before I was to visit my family in Los Angeles. I figured that while I was in L.A. I would go to the university on the off chance that he might be there. When I got to the psychology office and asked the receptionist if Dr. Goodman was available she laughed good-heartedly,

"He's never here."

I knew of one other professor at UCLA, Dr. Allen Parducci. I had read an article of his within the last year. Dr. Parducci was a cognitive psychologist and even though I had intended to apply in the clinical area I decided to take a shot anyway,

"Is Allen Parducci in?"

"He's right over there," she said pointing at the barrel-chested, white bearded gentleman checking his mail.

I went up to him and introduced myself. He graciously invited me up to his office, where we had a wide-ranging discussion covering philosophy, education, psychology, as well as his work. (His prime research interest was 'happiness.' Could it have gotten any better?) We hit it off and stayed in touch. I became a born-again cognitive psychologist and reapplied to UCLA. Eight months after that initial meeting I was accepted into the graduate school of psychology and was fortunate beyond measure to have had Allen as my advisor. I had a tremendous three years at the University. Oh, and by the way, in all that time I never saw Gerry Goodman.

This is the essence of adapting, finding alternate paths to the goal and/or alternate goals to fulfill the purpose. Given the fluid nature of life in the 21st century it is more necessary than ever for our kids to become adept at adapting. The new game is more purpose fulfillment than goal acquisition. The more ways your children can think of to express and fulfill their purposes, the more likely they will be to experience great lives.

And/Or Something Better

To help your children learn to be adaptable teach them to hold on to their purposes firmly, their goals lightly, and their plans more lightly still. When your children are young the easier you are about change, the more lightly you hold onto your own goals and plans, the easier your children will be and the lighter will be their grasp.

As they get older you can help them cultivate an intense ease in their approach to their goals. This is a very Zen concept. You want to help them go after their goals as if that goal was the most important thing in the world, while at the same time have it not matter whether or not they reach that goal. It is a powerful state to be in when a goal matters like life itself and, at the same instant, doesn't matter at all. It is a state such as this that will allow them to engage both fully and freely.

A friend of mine once told me that when he was a teenager he and his friends would play pickup touch football every weekend. Every so often there would be a play in the game over which they would have a mighty disagreement. They could have been arguing about whether a runner was inbounds or out of bounds; or if a receiver actually caught the ball. Sometimes an argument would go on for more than half an hour and even get to the point where he and his friends were about to come to blows. After much yelling and screaming, intense emotion, and arguing as if their lives depended on it they would call the game in frustration and anger. Within minutes as they were walking off the field they would all be laughing and planning their next group activity.

Way too often we are owned by our goals. We believe we **must** achieve them. We won't let them go, even if something better comes along. In fact, we can get so wrapped up in the pursuit of a goal that we won't even notice if something better comes up to us, taps us on the shoulder, and introduces itself. Rather than have their goals own them, we want to teach our daughters and sons how to own their goals, and own them freely.

One way to help them do this is to teach them to add four little words at the end of all their goal statements: **and/or something better.** For example, your daughter has a goal: 'To get a 3.5 GPA.' Having her add on those four words so her goal now becomes, 'To get a 3.5 GPA and/or something better,' will help keep her mind open to other possibilities. This may they seem like a very tiny thing, yet it has proved helpful to many, many people. By keeping the window of possibility opened a crack it increases their chances of noticing opportunities they might not have noticed if they were solely focused on their goal.

Another approach to helping your children have light grasps on their goals and plans is to teach them to create alternate plans. One plan isn't enough. When all our eggs are in one basket, freely and lightly holding that basket can become difficult; our tendency is to hold on as tightly as we can. Teaching your children to have a plan is very good; teaching them to have plans A, B, C, and D is much better. It's even better if plan B is preferable to plan A and plan C more preferable still. The greater number of paths your children can see to fulfill their purposes and accomplish their goals, the better they will do in a rapidly changing environment.

The Virtue of Persistence

> *"It's not that I'm so smart, it's just that I stay with problems longer."*
>
> Albert Einstein

Overnight successes are often decades in the making. Successful business people usually fail five or six times before they create a business that is successful. The difference between people who fail and those who succeed often comes down to where they stop. This is one of the great lessons for your children to learn.

Creative Problem Solving

Norvin Johnson is a fitness expert and martial arts master. When it comes to physical training, athletic conditioning, weight loss, and body sculpting he is the most educated and capable person I know. He is the founder of Fierce Fitness Kickboxing, a truly amazing fitness and wellness program in Portland, OR. (You can check him out at www.fiercefitness.com.)

Norvin and I go way back. We've been friends for 35 years. We met as students of my colleague, Dr. Jim Samuels in the mid-1970s. One day about 15 years ago, Jim wanted to do something for a good friend who needed more storage space. He offered to have a shed built for his friend and called Norvin who, in addition to being a fitness guru, is also pretty handy. He asked our friend if he would help him with a shed. Norvin was only too happy to lend a hand.

I had been looking for something to do that weekend and when I heard about the project I offered to join in. Jim would provide the resources, Norvin would provide his building expertise, and I would help with the construction. The whole thing shouldn't take more than a day or so. First thing in the morning Norvin went to price out some options and I went along for the ride. He determined that a 8' x 10' shed could be bought new for about $900 or built from scratch for about the same price.

We brought back this information to the benefactor who told us the size was right but he only wanted to put in $300, so would we go out and see what we could do. (And by we, of course I mean Norvin.) So, we went out again. Norv worked his magic and figured out how to build the shed for $610. We went back to Jim who once again told us that he wanted it done for $300. Out we went again. Working his special kind of magic Norv got the cost down to $450. This proved still not to be good enough and after two more tries not only did Norvin get the price down to $300, he had designed a bigger shed. We all had a great time getting the shed built the next day.

I had learned a most valuable lesson: if you keep looking for an answer, you're likely to find one. How do you build a shed for $300? That was the question for that weekend. There are many more interesting questions to answer. How can you provide for your family working eight hours a week? How does my daughter, an average student, go to college for free? You'll never know what paths can open to you until you seriously consider the question.

"But aren't some things impossible?" you ask. Perhaps. But how many times have you thought something impossible one day only to see someone doing it the next? What we judge to be possible or impossible, all too often, is limited by our beliefs. Paraphrasing Napoleon Hill, "What we can conceive and believe we can achieve." We simply need to pose the right questions and persist until we have the right answers.

Banging the Drum

I believe the term, 'banging the drum,' originated in China. I first heard it as a martial arts student. It is a metaphor for patient, persistent practice. If you do something long enough, you will become good at it. You don't even have to try. In fact, trying gets in the way. If your children simply put the time into their work, they will be successful. It's as easy as banging a drum.

Banging the drum reminds us to incorporate ease into our practice. The value of practicing easily cannot be overstated. Practicing easily allows you to persist longer. Practicing easily encourages lightness and fun. Too often parents seem to forget they're in it for the long run. They push their children intensely, taking the joy out of the activity, and so court burnout. It is longevity that has the greater chance of producing excellence, and it is ease that allows for longevity.

Improvement is what keeps kids motivated to continue banging their drum. Sometimes when your daughter has been practicing the piano for half an hour a day, five days a week it can be difficult for her to notice that she has improved. You can help. If you have the means, periodically make some recording of your daughter's work so she can see and/or hear how much better she is getting. If she ever feels discouraged because she believes she is not making progress, you can just roll the tape.

Being patient and persistent are tremendous attributes for your children to develop as they pursue their dreams. Often times success is simply a matter of being able to accept rejection and continuing to moving forward. Much of life is a numbers game. Every successful salesperson will tell you they have to get X amount of no's before they get a yes; and so whenever they get rejected they get excited because they know they are that much closer to a sale.

Your son wants a girlfriend? At one level all he needs to do is continue asking. Of course, it can only help his chances if he showers and dresses appropriately. His chances will be even better if he's goal oriented and a good listener. That being said, the greatest guitar player in the world will never work unless he is willing and able to persistently knock on a door looking for gig, have that door slammed in his face, and happily move on the next door. You want to teach your children to keep their heads in the game and continue pursuing whatever it is they want.

Advocating for Themselves

If your children are going to be successful they will need to learn how to stand up for themselves and interact well with people in authority. Fortunately, your kids have a great laboratory in which to develop these skills . . . school. There are so many lessons they can learn there that will serve them throughout their lives.

The phrase, 'advocating for yourself,' often has been tinged with a hint of conflict. There is a suggestion that you need to stand up for yourself against someone. While at times this is necessary, it is more useful to think of 'advocating for yourself' as a more cooperative effort. In school the students that learn to work with teachers, administrators, and the rest of the staff have a great advantage over those that haven't. Having the good will of all these people can be invaluable in a pinch. Situations arise all the time in which students can really use the support of a teacher, custodian, vice-principal, or administrative assistant.

First and foremost your daughters and sons need to understand that when they are in school it is their education. It is up to them to make the most of it. So, if there is something they don't understand, it is on them to ask their teachers for help. Many students do this readily, yet some students seem uncomfortable or reticent to go to their teachers for assistance. If your child is one of the latter you can help them at home through role-playing. Sit down with your child and discuss what it is s/he would like to say to or ask his teacher. When they are clear have them talk to you as if you were their teacher. With enough repetition your child will gain the confidence they need to interact well with anybody.

Students who ask teachers for help show that they're interested in the class. Simply showing interest often results in improved grades. Teachers love it when students are interested. So few students are actually interested in school these days that when a student shows genuine interest their teacher takes a greater interest in them; and if at the end of the term that student has a high B the teacher will often find a way to turn that high B into an A. It's just human nature. We enjoy helping people we like.

The surest way for your son or daughter to get a teacher on their side is to be interested in class. Another way is for them to be respectful of the teacher's time. Toward the end of the grading period there are always a number of students who rush the teacher to find out their grades. If their grades are not high enough, they see what work needs to be made up or what extra credit they could turn in to improve them. These students are being quite disrespectful and while many teachers are willing to help, many teachers feel a little put out . . . and they should. This is very much like someone asking you for a recommendation and telling you they need it this afternoon. Students who do this demonstrate that they are solely interested in their grades and have little interest in the subject or the teacher.

Teachers are much more appreciative of students who check on their progress periodically throughout the term, and they are much happier providing these students with opportunities to raise their grades. Every three weeks or so your daughter or son, especially if s/he is in middle school or above, should be checking in with their teachers to see where they stand. This is another way for students to positively interact with their teachers and advocate for themselves.

Yet another way for students to get teachers and others on their side is simply to show their appreciation. Thank them every now and then. This small graciousness, genuinely expressed, will go a long way. This also goes for you, the parents. They only time most teachers and parents interact is when something is wrong; and too many of these interactions tend to be adversarial. So, when teachers see parents coming they can get defensive. This does not have to be the case.

By having positive interactions with your child's teachers you can almost guarantee mutual cooperation if the time comes when something serious needs to be addressed. Every so often, when your child is excited about a lesson or finally understands something they've been struggling with, send the teacher a little thank you note. Not only will they will really appreciate it, they will see you as an ally.

Why have I just spent a couple of pages talking about building alliances with teachers and school staff? Simple. It is much easier and more effective advocating for oneself with friends and allies. Things are so much more likely to go your way. It's true, sometimes there is a need to advocate for oneself in a seemingly hostile environment. However, if you teach your children to prepare the ground before hand through building strong relationships, that need will likely never manifest. If you teach your children to be appreciative and respectful, they will have great success negotiating on their own behalf.

Student Interlude

Making Teachers Your Allies

His name was Bruce. The summer over, he was preparing for his junior year. As he looked over his schedule he noticed he had the toughest English teacher in the school. He didn't mind too much because she also had the reputation of being one of the best teachers in the school. Students who worked with her significantly improved their writing skills. Bruce was actually looking forward to this, realizing that college was less than two years away and he knew his skills needed work.

During the first week of school his teacher handed the class their first writing assignment and by the second week she had returned it to the students marked up and graded. Bruce received a C, as did most of the other guys in the class. Most of the girls received A's and B's. The next week's assignment went the same way, boys got C's and girls got A's and B's. Bruce believed this could not be a coincidence and went about figuring what to do for the next assignment. Then it hit him.

For the next assignment Bruce decided to respond as he imagined a girl would respond. He received the first of many A's. He had learned a valuable lesson: give them what they want.

Teachers are human too. We humans like it when others share our viewpoints. Sure there are teachers who prefer a spirited argument and if you have such a teacher, please argue spiritedly. The game is to find out what they respond most favorably to and give it to them to the best of your ability. This is one way to make the teacher your ally.

There were many others. Be interested in class, contribute to discussions, ask questions, hand your assignments in on time, anything that demonstrates you're interested in the subject. The reason why Mr. Jones teaches biology is because he actually likes biology and thinks it's valuable. The reason why Mrs. Smith teaches calculus is because she actually finds calculus exciting. Little gets a teacher's juices flowing more than a student who is interested in learning. It's why they became a teacher in the first place.

Making your teachers your allies can be worth half a grade to you. If you are sitting between a B+ and an A, and your teacher likes you, he will likely find a way to give you the A. Demonstrating you are interested in class is easy. You're in class anyway; you might as well pay attention. You don't have to suck up to the teacher or even do any extra credit assignments. You simply have to take an interest in what they are teaching.

Chapter Eight

Connecting:

Building Meaningful Relationships

We can live without religion and meditation, but we cannot survive without human affection.

H. H. the Dalai Lama

It seems to me that trying to live without friends is like milking a bear to get cream for your morning coffee. It is a whole lot of trouble, and then not worth much after you get it.

Zora Neale Hurston

In large part the quality of our lives is dependent upon the quality of our relationships. If our children are going to look back upon rich lives, they will do so because of the love they have exchanged with people close to them. Building meaningful relationships is a skill, not a given. I know a number of people who, by midlife, have few if any meaningful, close relationships outside of their family. Some of them got too wrapped up in their work. Others got too wrapped up in their families. Either way they did not maintain and grow their early friendships, nor did they take the time to create new ones.

Today, there is a new player in the game that is affecting our children's relationship building: technology. Facebook, MySpace, texting, tweeting, all are impacting the way our children relate with each other, the nature of which we will not know for a number of years. On the face of it the quantity of communication has vastly increased while the depth of communication may have diminished severely. I know many twenty-somethings who have few, if any people to confide in outside of their families. As with midlifers who have few friends, I believe their lives may be lacking.

Deep, close relationships are one of the building blocks of happy and healthy lives. To create and enjoy these relationships it would help to understand the components of friendship; be able to be an exceptional communicator, (communication is the cement with which friendships are built), and know what it takes to maintain and grow intimacy.

The Recipe for Friendship

All too often our children befriend the wrong people. They befriend kids who just intend to use them for their own ends. They become friends with kids who will throw them under the bus at the first sign of trouble. They make friends with kids who are simply not healthy. It is important that our children learn what good and true friendship really is.

Friendship is one of those terms that we tend to define very ambiguously, and it is due to this ambiguity that we can be surprised and a bit confused when someone we thought was a friend turns out to be otherwise. Perhaps it's because we tend to define friendship in terms of feelings, and while feelings certainly are important in friendship, only using them to guide us doesn't necessarily enhance our understanding or clarity.

So, how can we think about friendship a bit more objectively? Friendship can be considered to be made up of three ingredients: knowing, liking, and trusting. All of these are necessary for people to be friends. Helping our children understand what makes a

friend a friend will enable them to become good friends and identify people with whom good friendships are possible.

Knowing

Friends know each other. They know each other's weaknesses
and strengths, they know where they each fall short and they know
where they can count on each other. Becoming friends first and
foremost is all about getting to know each other. This means your
children have to be knowable. They have to be willing to show
people who and what they are. Encourage your sons and daughters to confidently be themselves and teach them what to look for
in their peers.

Liking

For people to be friends they need to like each other and they
need to be enough alike. There needs to be enough agreement as
to how they see the world, or at least a part of it. They could be
interested in similar things. They could like doing similar things.
They could share the same political or spiritual outlook. They
could be like-minded. They could be kindred spirits. There simply
needs to be something that draws them together, a reason to enjoy
each other's company.

In order to be a good friend your son or daughter needs to be
able to find qualities in others that they like. Listen to the conversations they have with their peers. Do they tear down others
or build them up? How many adults do you know who seem to
look for the negative in people and situations? They usually find a
reason something won't work or some activity won't be fun. They
spend a considerable amount of time ragging on family members,
fellow workers, or people at their place of worship. Talk with
them and you have hard time finding much that they like in the
world. They learned to do this as children.

Your children need to find the good, the enjoyable, the admirable in people and events. If your children do not do this naturally, you will have to teach them. Asking them to identify these qualities regularly will help them establish the habit of doing so. When you hear them complaining about some situation, ask them what is enjoyable about it. When you hear them put down another, ask them what is admirable about that person. Do not take, "I don't know," for an answer. Keep persisting until they are successful. Teaching them to find the positive will make it easier for them to like others and at the same time make them more likeable.

Trusting

The final ingredient for friendship is trust. Your sons and daughters need to be trustworthy and they need to have friends they can trust. Trust boils down to two factors. First, are you truthful? Second, do you keep your agreements? If your children are to be trustworthy, they must be truthful. Good friends both are truthful and keep their agreements.

To be truthful they must be both honest and accurate. One will not do; truth is made up of both. An eyewitness might be very honest and report what they saw. However, if they misunderstood what they saw or only saw a part of an event, they would not be wholly accurate, and so their report would not be true. Similarly, another person might have seen the entire event and not report honestly. Their report would also not be true. It takes both. Of course, all good parents endeavor to teach their children to be both accurate and honest.

Do you make clear agreements with your children and hold them to those agreements? Do you follow through on your agreements? This is not only important to build their trustworthiness, it is important because only people who keep their agreements can actually demand that others do the same. The best advice I ever got as to making agreements came from my mentor: "Only make those agreements you can keep. Even better, only make those agreements you can keep easily."

"I will love you forever." Whether you are aware of it or not that is an agreement, an agreement, which, by the way, is almost impossible to keep. Please do not accept commitments from your children to "be good from now on," "turn all my homework in on time for the rest of the year," or some such long-term statement of purpose or goal. You will only be helping them set themselves up for failure, as well as the guilt that most of us experience when we break our word. Much better that you put time limits on these commitments, time limits that give your kids a good chance to be successful. Doing so will help your children develop their trustworthiness.

Knowing, liking, and trusting are the prime ingredients with which to build a friendship. The more knowable, likable, and trustworthy your children are the better friend they will be and the better chance they will have of finding people with whom they can develop healthy, deep, lifelong friendships.

Communication: The Glue of Friendship

It is through communication that we build our friendships. Teaching our children to be good communicators is one of the more wondrous gifts we can bestow upon them. In order to be good communicators we need to help them develop five specific skills:

1. Being present
2. Listening
3. Being patient
4. Clearly getting their ideas across to others
5. Reading body language

Being Present

Being present refers to being there for people and looking someone in the eye when you speak. In all the different kinds of relationships your children will be a party to, the ability to look at someone when they're talking will serve them extremely well. Whether we are transacting business, exploring a physically intimate relationship, or building a friendship, we like people to look at us.

The more attention your children can bring to an interaction, the better the odds they have of making it go well. You can help their development in a number of ways. Make sure you have them practice looking at you when they speak. Similarly, when they're talking with others, if you notice them talking to the ground, encourage them to look up. Certainly, when you or anyone else is talking to them, encourage them to look at the speaker. If your child is shy, encourage them gently . . . and persistently.

Looking at people when we are communicating is important; paying attention is even more so. When you were a kid you probably played 'staring' games with your friends. The goal was to look each other in the eye and the last one to move was the winner. Friends who got good at this game did so by focusing their thoughts on anything but the person in front of them. They might sing songs to themselves, think about boring things, count sheep, anything other than 'being there.'

This is the exact opposite of being present. So, it is important that you train your daughter to pay attention as she is communicating. You can do this simply by asking her what was just said. You can turn it into a game. Sit across from her and subtly move your body and see if she can notice and tell you what you did. Raise your eyebrow, move your finger, nod your head, flare your nostrils, wiggle your ears if you can. Continue playing until she can notice the most subtle of movements. Feel free to change roles and see if you can notice her movements. It's fun.

Beyond communication, 'being there' has a larger connotation: actually being there for our friends when it counts. We instinctually know how valuable this is from an early age. Teenagers find it so important for them to be there in support of their family and friends. Most kids want to make a difference in other people's lives and any time they are aware of an opportunity they tend to step up. Throughout our lives it's being there when it counts that truly strengthens the bonds of friendship.

Listening

We all teach our kids to listen. The question is what do we teach them to listen for? If the purpose is to build close relationships, we want to teach them to listen for ways to contribute to their friend's world. This means listening for their friend's purposes and goals. Knowing their friend's purposes and goals will give them clearer insight as to how to best support them. The more support they can contribute, the cooler friend there are. Your daughters and sons need to learn to keep an ear out for any opportunity to make their friends' lives better.

Ever have to repeat something half a dozen times to your son and still weren't sure whether or not he heard you? As part of teaching your kids to listen it is important that you teach them to let the person talking know they were listening. When a person is through talking a simple 'Okay,' 'Fine,' 'Good,' 'Thanks, I got it,' will let the other know they were heard. Anything that lets the speaker know they were listening will do. Developing this habit in your family will may make communicating go much smoother.

Being Patient

We want to teach our kids to give people time to formulate their thoughts. Their friends will value them for this granting of time and they will value them more as they get older. Being patient is closely connected to listening, and both of these are closely connected to being present. In times of great stress having a friend who will be there and patiently listen to us sort things out can be worth more than gold.

Being Clear

Saying what they mean and meaning what they say. This is the essence of communicating clearly. If your children are going to enjoy the kinds of relationships you hope for them, they will do well to learn to communicate directly, gracefully, and tactfully. You can go a long way to ensure that your children are capable of simply communicating their wants and intentions. At times they will do this with words, at other times with actions. Either way, the more directly and clearly they can put their ideas out there, the better chance they have of being successful.

You can also teach them to get their ideas across in ways that make it as easy as possible for others to understand and accept. It's one thing to tell your friend they're out of line. It's another thing to tell them in such a way that they can hear it and perhaps explore changing their behavior. In every friendship there are moments of disagreement as well as moments of misunderstanding. If your children learn to communicate tactfully, these moments will be smoothed over readily.

Teaching your sons and daughters to communicate clearly is fairly straightforward and can be a lot of fun. If your daughter has heard that a person who she has considered to be a friend is talking about her behind her back, it certainly would be best for your daughter to speak with her friend and find out what is really going on.

That conversation can have many outcomes, depending on your daughter's approach. What outcome would she prefer? What will she say and how will she say it? What attitude will she bring to the conversation? These are all questions you can explore with her. Have her try speaking her piece a number of different ways, from various attitudes, until she discovers the approach that will work best for her. Once she has settled on her approach, you and she can practice saying what she wants, as well as saying it from the attitude she has chosen. Keep practicing until she is confident. As with learning any skill, practice is the key.

Paying Attention to Body Language

Teaching your children to pay attention to body language can give them great insights into the intentions and interests of others. There have been a number of books written addressing the language of the body, some of them very intricate and involved. For our purposes, we will keep it very simple. You want to teach your children to identify when someone is retreating or reaching. Simply retreating or reaching.

If someone is retreating from a communication they don't like the idea; if they are reaching, they do. Retreats and reaches range from obvious to subtle. An obvious retreat may be actually stepping backwards. A slightly less obvious one may be the folding of one's arms or crossing one's legs. A more subtle one could be a lowering of the voice. Nodding one's head is a pretty obvious reach, as is smiling. A pupil dilating is a much more subtle one.

Subtle or obvious, noticing retreats and reaches can provide us with valuable information. For the purposes of building close, meaningful relationships paying attention to our friends' body language can help us better support them. Let's say, for example, your son and his girlfriend are deciding what to do on Saturday evening. Your son suggests going to a movie. His girlfriend, wanting to be agreeable, says okay, but in a noncommittal tone of voice. If your son is sharp he'll notice that she just retreated from the idea of going to a movie and suggest something else. He will keep suggesting ideas until there is one his girlfriend clearly reaches on. Now they're both guaranteed to have a better time.

The more important the issue, the more value there is in paying attention to body language. Think about your own lives. Have your friends ever saved you from making a big mistake because of what they saw in you? Have you ever had a friend tell you that 'something about you doesn't seem right ever since you began thinking about taking that new job?' Then you find that after some careful consideration the job really is wrong for you.

Being there, listening, being patient, being clear, paying attention to body language all comprise the mortar with which close friendships are built, grown, and maintained. Encouraging your children to develop these skills will significantly improve their chances of having the kinds of relationships that make their lives rich and enjoyable.

Making Friends

Some of our children are naturally gregarious, outgoing, and socially adept. Their peers are attracted to them; they make friends readily, and are seemingly comfortable in any situation. Some of our children are quite the opposite. They are shy, uncomfortable around people they do not know, and find it difficult to make friends. Once they do make a friend, however, they are able to establish strong bonds with them.

What these kids seem to need the most is to develop the skill of meeting people. Whether our kids are outgoing or shy, this particular skill is a good one for them to learn. It is also pretty simple. In order to meet people all they need to do is build up the courage to say hello, say their name, and ask questions. That's all there is to it. People of every age love talking about themselves. All our sons and daughters need to be able to do is get people to talk about themselves and then pay attention to the answers.

It begins with an introduction. As an adult it is striking when a young person confidently comes up, looks me in the eye, shakes my hand, and tells me his name. Only slightly more impressive is when he asks me mine. Teaching them how to shake hands and introduce themselves, then practicing with them, will help them develop the confidence to go out and do it themselves. Make sure you have them practice introducing themselves to their peers in the manner in which they actually do so.

Once they can confidently introduce themselves, move onto the next step: helping them develop questions to ask and giving them practice asking them. Most kids are quite good at coming up with questions after just a little assistance. These questions should be simple and geared towards encouraging others to talk about themselves. "Where are you from?" "What school do you go to?" "What kind of music do you like?" "What do you do for fun?" "Where is your family from?" "Do you have any brothers or sisters?" "Do you game?" "Do you play sports?" "Do you play music?" Anything to get them talking. From there, whenever they feel comfortable they can start asking about the other person's goals and plans for the future. All they have to do is listen. Things will occur naturally from there.

With just a little rehearsal followed by some real-world practice, kids will become much more comfortable in social settings. This is great for shy kids to learn for obvious reasons. It is also great for outgoing kids as well. Many gregarious kids are very good at talking about themselves and not as good at listening to others. Making friends is more about listening than talking.

Developing Closeness

> *An old friend will help you move. A good friend will help you move a dead body.*
>
> Jim Hayes

Rarely do we remain close with our friends from childhood. When we do, these relationships are very special. In elementary school we have friends by default. Our friends are made up of kids that live nearby, kids that we meet in programs that our parents enroll us in, and kids in our school class. It is in middle school and high school that we begin to choose our friends for ourselves and begin to become aware of the possibility of doing things for our friendships. It is in our teens that we become aware that our actions can separate us from our friends or bring us closer to them.

Being There

Being there is in part about simply showing up and sharing our lives over time. Close, meaningful relationships tend to be built over the long haul. Being there for the bad, the good, and the mundane are all part of developing closeness. It rarely matters what we do together so long as we doing it with each other. We certainly don't have to do anything special; being together is enough.

Another aspect of being there is stepping up when it matters. Over the course of our lives we hold special places in our hearts for those people who stepped up to the plate and were there when it mattered. We all have friends with whom we go out, share kid duties, go on vacations, and do business. But of all those people, how many show up when the doodoo hits the fan? Those we number among our close friends.

Providing our young children opportunities to be there when it counts not only will help them make a difference, it will also increase their self-esteem. Encouraging our teenagers to go to the aid of their friends when they believe they are in need will help them thicken the bonds of their friendship and make them better able to be friends with others in the future.

Appreciation

Being there is not enough. Becoming closer also involves showing appreciation to those we care for. Thanking people for their help and support is cool, as is thanking them for a birthday gift. However, being appreciative entails more than just saying thank you upon receiving a gift or upon receiving help from a friend.

Appreciation actually means to improve the value of something. To appreciate means to make more valuable. If we are to appreciate our friends we need to make them more valuable. Increasing each other's value is one way that the bonds of friendship are strengthened. How do your children make their friends more valuable? They help their friends achieve their goals. They help them become better people. They help them do things that contribute to their families and communities.

This may seem like a pretty tall order. Actually it can be quite simple. Helping their friend to do their homework is an act of appreciation. Encouraging their friend to talk to that guy she is interested in is also an act of appreciation; as is pushing their friend to be truthful with his parents. Listening to their friend when they are troubled, teaching them how eat a little more healthfully, helping their friends do their chores are all acts of appreciation. Helping our children find ways to increase the value of their friends will, once again, increase their own assessment of their self-worth, while at the same time enhancing the quality of their friendships.

In second grade my friend Gilbert decided that throughout his schooling he would offer to help anyone in need with their school work. Gilbert was the most academically gifted student in our class of pretty academically gifted kids. He seemed to have a sense that super smart kids were often ostracized by their peers. Gil helped us all at one time or another. He was great!. In junior high school, a time when a number of the really 'bright' kids found trouble at the hands of those not nearly as academically gifted, Gilbert was one of the most beloved students in the school.

The tough kids never picked on him; to the contrary, many of them protected him. He helped any of them who asked, and before the cynics among you think, "Sure, he did their homework for them," let me assure you Gilbert had ethical standards. He would never help them cheat, he would just help them learn. He carried his commitment all the way through medical school, increasing the value of dozens, perhaps hundreds of students along the way. Today, I am honored to number him amongst my closest friends. As of the writing of this book we've been close for about 43 years.

Love

Of course, closeness cannot be developed without love. In fact, closeness in part defines love. Think about what love means. Love is a deep feeling for someone or something. Love is a feeling of warm personal attachment or deep affection. Love is an intense emotional attraction to someone or something. These are good definitions. However, while they tell us what love is, they do not give us many clues as to how to love.

A definition of love I have found most useful: love is consistent demonstrations of consideration. Consistent demonstrations of consideration. I like this definition so much, dare I say love it, because it describes how to love. I think we all have a sense that saying, 'I love you,' while certainly nice to hear from someone we care for, in and of itself does not quite do it for us. We need more, and the more would be consistent demonstrations of consideration.

When we love somebody not only do we think about them often, we demonstrate that we are doing so. So, when your children tell you they love you, hug and kiss them, and every so often ask them to prove it. Ask them to show you. We want to teach our children that loving requires more than words, it requires deeds. When your son feels 'in love' with his high school sweetheart, help him find ways to consistently show her he is thinking about her. Flowers are always special. Knowing her goals and helping her achieve them are even more so. Teaching our kids how to love is paramount if they are to have love and give love in their lives.

Keeping it Together

Building relationships is one thing; maintaining them is quite another. At the opening of this book I mentioned the importance of having strong, truthful, open lines of communication between you and your children. Strong, truthful, and open communication is what builds and maintains intimacy between us. When the communication lines are free and clear we become, and remain, as close as we can be. We become distant from each other when the lines get muddied. If the lines get obstructed enough we may separate.

Most of us have seen it happen. Our friend meets that special person. As they are falling in love we hear how wonderful s/he is. We watch the couple and they seem quite well suited for each other. After a year or two they marry and for a while things are very good. Then, little by little, the complaints start. In a few years we hear bitterness in our friend's voice. Six years into their marriage they divorce. What happened? Though every relationship is different, underlying the trouble you will most likely find poor, muddied and/or closed communication lines. If you notice your son becoming more distant, the lines of communication between the two of you have probably been compromised. You can bet there is something he is not telling you. If your daughter and her best friend are no longer hanging out with each other, there is almost certainly something someone doesn't want the other to find out.

Keeping the Lines Free and Clear

Communication flows free and clear so long as there is truth. Waters get muddied when the truth is jeopardized. Remember, truth is comprised of both honesty and accuracy. To the degree that either of those are diminished, the lines of communication become muddy and the relationship becomes more distant. People aren't truthful for a number of reasons, a few of them well-intentioned and even altruistic.

Often kids are not truthful because they don't want to experience some consequence or another. They might not like to be the target of their parent's anger. They might not like to have someone they care for think less of them. They might be trying not to hurt a someone's feelings. They may even believe the truth will really damage someone they love, so they hide it. Sometimes they're not truthful because they're too inhibited; they are just too uncomfortable talking about a subject. Other times they're not entirely truthful simply because they believe the issue at hand is too trivial to bring up. Regardless of the reason, the less truth, the greater the distance; the more truth, the greater the closeness.

By the way, this also goes for parents. There are times that it's the parents who are less than completely truthful. In relationships, of all types, when there is trouble, it's a pretty safe bet it has been a team effort.

Whether you are working to build a new relationship, repair an existing relationship that was once close, or grow a good relationship into a great one that will stand the test of time, you must keep the lines free and clear. Here I will show you a method of doing so. This method can be used in any kind of relationship to great effect. Teach your daughter or son to use it by using it with them; then teach them how to use it with their friends. With practice not only will they be able to use it with those they care for, they will gain a much greater understanding of the dynamics of the relationships around them.

The Four Magic Questions (Samuels)

In this exercise you will need to apply the communication skills presented earlier in this chapter. The more you can be present, listen and let your partner know s/he has been heard, be patient, clearly communicate, and pay attention to their body language, they greater success you will have. If you are going to make this work you will also need to follow some very simple rules that can at times require a great amount of self-discipline.

Rule #1: Get your partner's agreement.

Whether you are doing this exercise with your son, daughter, mother, father, friend, significant other, business partner, or mate, all parties need to agree to participate in good faith. Please do not 'spring' this on someone or try to coerce them into doing it. I have seen the results and they rarely are pretty. Getting everyone's agreement will give all concerned the best chance to be successful.

Rule #2: Follow the pattern: stick to the questions.

Have one person (A) begin by asking the other (B) all four questions, one at a time. When B has finished answering them, switch; have B ask A the questions. **Do not improvise! For best results ask the questions as they are written.**

Rule #3: Let your partner know they have been heard.

When your daughter has answered a question let her know you have heard her by responding with 'Okay,' 'Fine,' 'Good,' 'Thanks, I got it,' or some such indication you received what they said.

Rule #4: Shut up. Anything goes.

When you are the one asking the questions you must simply listen to your son's answers and let him know they have been heard. You must not make any comment! You must not argue! You must not help to clarify! **You must simply listen.** This is the most crucial rule. I cannot emphasize this enough. Trust me, the amount of self-discipline it can take when your son accuses you of something you know you did not do can be enormous. If you feel you need a referee, feel free to ask someone, perhaps another family member, to help keep you both on track.

Rule #5: It's over when it is over.

You know you are done when you and your daughter answer, "No," to all the questions. It will take as long as it takes. I have helped numerous couples with this exercise. Those who have been together a long time, who have had the habit of stuffing their feelings rather than communicating, have taken hours to complete this exercise. Sometimes we have had to work in stages, taking a chunk at a time. More often, pairs who have had a tradition of fairly open communication can complete the exercise in under an hour. Those who do this exercise routinely, once a week or twice a month, can often complete it in fifteen minutes or so. Take your time and take as long as you need. It will be well worth it.

The Four Magic Questions
1. Is there anything I have done that wasn't OK?
2. Is there anything I failed to do that I should have done?
3. Is there anything you did that wasn't OK?
4. Is there anything you failed to do that you should have done?

Running this exercise will bring more truth to your relationships and so help them grow into the best relationships they are capable of being. Please be aware that simply doing this exercise will not guarantee that you and your son will agree on all fronts. In a small percentage of instances people find that they really do have significant areas of disagreement. If that is the truth, so be it. In the vast majority of instances though, the participants experience much greater understanding and closeness. If your kids learn how to do this with you and their friends, they will have greatly enhanced their ability to create meaningful, deep, life-long friendships.

Study after study reports that longevity and quality of life are largely dependent on the bonds of friendship and love we create. Understanding what friendship is about, being a good friend and knowing friendship when they see it; knowing how to communicate and being able to do so with confidence; being able to build intimacy; these, much more than material gain, are at the heart of a rich life. If you are to ensure such wealth for your children, you will have to do your best to teach them how to create such bonds and maintain them throughout their lives.

Making Your Mark

If you are reading this you are no longer a child. You aren't quite an adult yet either. You are growing into your adulthood. As you become your own person, what qualities would you like to be known for? Will you be known for your loyalty? Will you be known for your kindness? Will you be known for your persistence? Will you be known for your friendship? What will you be known for? What mark will you leave on the world?

You are coming into your adulthood in a world that is in some pretty deep sewage. Climate change, population growth, worldwide debt, fundamentalist fanaticism, threats to air and water, compromised health around the world, the list goes on. Your generation will be facing many serious problems. The good news is that with problems come opportunities and the bigger the problems the greater the opportunities.

Your generation will have some mighty, mighty big opportunities. You all have some decisions to make. The first will be where will you put your attention, on the problem or on solutions and opportunities? Some of your peers complain about the way things are. They either believe they cannot change things or would rather not spend the energy to try. They have decided to focus on the problems. Others of your peers work to improve things. They believe they can make a difference.

They are the ones focused on solutions and opportunities. *Which one are you? Which one would you like to be?*

If you have decided to join the forces for improvement the next decision before you is, what will your mark be? This is a question I hope you'll ask yourselves many times throughout your life. You are not expected to come up with THE ANSWER; you are young and don't have that much life experience. However, you can come up with AN ANSWER and can explore the possibilities for the longer-term. You can look for ways to leave your mark on your family, your friends, your school, and your community.

After working with young men and women for the last 20 years I am more convinced than ever that your generation can be the greatest to have graced our planet. You bring much to the table that is new and extremely valuable. Your ease and facility with technology, your ability and desire to work with others, your willingness to challenge and question assumptions, and your creativity all serve as a strong foundation from which many of the problems facing humanity can be solved.

Above all, your acceptance of, and empathy with, those who are different from you gives me confidence that my generation will leave the world in good hands.

What part will you play?

Chapter Nine

Making It Happen:
Developing Self Discipline

What we do upon some great occasion will probably depend on what we already are: and what we are will be the result of previous years of self-discipline.

H. P. Liddon

Being able to determine and maintain one's attitude; being able to set goals, plan, and manage resources; being able to think critically, persist, communicate, and adapt. These are the tools that lay the foundation for becoming extraordinary. If our children leave our homes with these in hand they will be well on their way to enjoying great lives.

There is, however, one more, piece to the puzzle. Our children must have the self-discipline to use these tools. One of the most important skills parents can pass on to their offspring is the ability to discipline themselves.

Discipline

So what is discipline? The other day I was working with a group of about 35 teenagers and asked them.

"Something that happens when you're bad."

"Punishment."

"What principals do."

"Someone being hard on you."

So discipline is a negative force imposed upon you. This is how most teens understand the idea of discipline. I've asked many adults this question and have often got very similar answers . . . and these answers are far from the mark.

Discipline means to follow or stay on a path. That's it. To follow or stay on a path to some destination. So how did we get all this distance between how our kids and many adults conceive of discipline and its core meaning? All good parents 'discipline' their children . . . with good reasons almost all of the time. Parents 'discipline' their children to teach them lessons, to help them walk a path. My parents were no different. Though when I was growing up and being 'disciplined' by my parents I do not recall understanding the path they were helping me to walk. They might have told me, I probably had my attention focused elsewhere. I know, in this regard, my childhood was not particularly unusual.

It is certainly important that you discipline your children; it is equally important that they understand the place to which you are leading them and the path you are encouraging them to take.

Perhaps it's even more important to expose them to positive discipline. I never learned that there were positive experiences of discipline, even though I experienced them with great frequency. Validation is a form of positive discipline. Material rewards are forms of positive discipline. So are hugs, kisses, and smiles. Even though at times we may not be aware we are doing so, we use all of these to help our kids stay on the straight and narrow.

I am well aware that there are times when harsher forms of discipline are necessary. Scolding, timeouts, a swat on the behind, stern looks, and groundings all have their place. I just strongly suggest that you do whatever is necessary to ensure that your children understand the destination and the path. In this way you will be helping them to have a more functional understanding of discipline. As with many of the other skills being discussed in this book this training can start at a very young age.

When my friend's daughter was about two years old he had to take her to the doctor for a check up. He told his daughter they would be leaving shortly and asked her to get her shoes ready. When she didn't move he asked her one more time, and when she continued to refuse to do as she was asked my friend waited a couple of minutes, said goodbye to her, and left her alone in the house. Before you start screaming child endangerment and abandonment, my friend only got in his car and moved it to where his daughter couldn't see him, all the while keeping a close eye on the house. After about fifteen minutes he went back in the house and got his daughter who was obviously very upset. As they were driving to the doctor's office they talked about what just happened. His daughter was much more cooperative from then on.

A key component of developing children who are disciplined is teaching them to obey. When our kids are young this word is usually quite acceptable to them. As many of our kids move into their teen years this word can become anathema. Why is that? I maintain that most teenagers and many people do not understand the true value of obedience.

Again, I have asked thousands of teens, "Why it is important to obey?" Their responses, though considerably better than those regarding discipline, still miss the mark. In all my years of asking this question only one student has hit the nail on the head. When asked the importance of obedience teens typically respond with,

"To learn from people who know more than you."

"To keep yourself safe."

"It's right to obey your elders."

"To have things go better."

Once again, their responses are not substantially different from the responses of most adults I have asked. Yes, these responses are all correct . . . and they are missing a very vital element. You see, the most important reason for them to learn to obey is that once they leave their parent's home, whether they are off to college or the workforce, the primary person they will have to obey is themselves. They will be the one responsible for getting themselves out of bed. They will be the one responsible for doing their work. They will be the one responsible for doing things they might not like where needed. If they do not develop the ability to take orders from themselves, they seriously damage their chances for success. It is with the practice of obeying their parents, teachers, and other authorities in their life that they develop their ability to obey themselves.

Which brings us to . . .

Self-Discipline

Self-discipline is following a path you set toward a destination of your choosing. Self-discipline involves developing the skills necessary to keep yourself on the path you choose. A few chapters ago we explored teaching your children how to choose destinations and set paths: goal setting and planning. Now let's look at some things you can do to help them develop their ability to walk their chosen path.

You, Your Mind, and Your Body

> *All right everyone, line up alphabetically according to your height.*

Casey Stengel

More than anything else, self-discipline is an act of will. Our will is the most powerful tool we have, and to make the best use of it we need to understand where it comes from. To do so we need to understand the players and their relationship to each other. The key players are you, your mind, and your body.

Let's start with your body. You have a body? Of course you do. Are you aware that you are not your body? You probably are. You are senior to your body. Have you ever had some important work to do, felt awful, and powered your way through anyway? That's an example of you running the show, being senior to your body. So, once again, you are not your body. You are connected to it, you are strongly influenced by it, and you are something other than it.

How about your mind. You have a mind? Of course you do. So what is this mind that you have? Tomes have been written in answer to this question. Let's keep it simple. Your mind is a thinking machine and when it works in conjunction with your body it is also a feeling/emoting machine. It is comprised of everything you have experienced, all the things you've learned, all the things you have thought, all the things you have felt. It also contains all your imaginings about possible futures. For most of us it is active all the time to some degree. Primarily it works by association.

You are not your mind. As with your body, you are senior to it. Have you ever received bad news that disturbed your equilibrium right before you had a major talk to give or meeting to attend, put that entire disturbance aside, and performed well? That was you being senior to your mind. Have you ever known someone, perhaps yourself, who was all out of sorts about something when they found out their child was in an accident? I bet they immediately were able to put all that stuff aside and be right there, ready and able to take care of their daughter or son.

Please understand, many of the thoughts in our minds are, and at the same time, are not ours. They are ours to the extent that they occurred in our mind. They are not to the extent that we did not intentionally think them. We have many thoughts that we did not intend to think. These thoughts seem to just arise. Have you ever been walking down the street and have a thought pop into your head? We all have. You did not intend to think this thought. It's not the same as the thinking you do to try to solve a problem, compose a letter, or come up with the most romantic way to propose to your fiancé.

Where do these random thoughts come from? They could have been triggered by something we saw, something we heard, something we felt, ate, smelled, or touched. Minds being great association machines, many thoughts are triggered by other thoughts.

Whatever the activity, we are senior to our mind. We are connected to it, we are strongly influenced by it, and we are something other than it. For the most part we interact with the universe through our mind. So, if we are not our body and we are not our mind, what are we? Have you ever watched yourself go through an experience? You are the watcher, the one that does the looking. When we step outside of ourselves and observe what we are doing, we are the observer.

What we are has been called many things by many people. We have been called spirit, soul, life force, energy, consciousness, child of God, and these are just a few. Regardless of the name, we are the animating principle; we are the thing that gives our body life. If you have ever seen a lifeless body, we are that thing that you can tell is not present when you're looking at it. You've heard the expression: 'The lights are on but nobody's home?' When somebody gets home, that's us. We all know when somebody is really present. It's this presence that we're talking about . . . and we are that presence.

If we so choose, we can run our own shows. We are the ones that can choose to express any attitude we desire. We are the ones that can choose to pursue any goal we desire. We are the ones that can, literally, change our minds for any reason and for no reason. We can take any viewpoint we wish and create any thought we can consider. The primary tool we have with which to do any or all of the above is our will, and will is also the primary tool we use to develop our self-discipline.

Disciplining One's Self

Nowhere is the ability to differentiate between you, your mind, and your body more important than in the development of self-discipline. Self-discipline is following a path you set towards a destination of your choosing. A self-disciplined person is one who can decide what s/he is going to do, then make it happen. In order to do this gracefully you, your mind, and your body need to be on the same page, all pulling in the same direction. If you are clear as to the difference between these players, exerting your will and placing your disciplinary efforts correctly will be much easier.

Have you ever decided that you were going to work out Saturday morning, only to find that when the alarm clock rang you were thinking, "Nah, I could go Sunday," or "I'd much rather drink coffee and read the newspaper." If something like this has ever happened to you, you were experiencing your mind being uncooperative. You had thoughts that ran counter to your intentions.

Have you ever not felt like doing what you had planned to do the day before? If you have, you experienced what it's like to have your mind and body be uncooperative, that is, you had thoughts and feelings that ran counter to your intentions. The goal of disciplining ourselves is to bring our mind and body in line with our intentions, goals and plans.

In most situations we all know what to do, we know what is right for us, and we know what will work best. However, sometimes we have urges (body), supported by reasons (mind), to do otherwise. We know we should exercise more. We know we should eat properly. We know we should take more time for our families. We know we shouldn't smoke and we know we could probably drink a little less. We know we should be more forgiving, and we know we should be more caring. Whatever you are contemplating, you almost always know what is right. Doing what is right is often another matter.

Our children are very much the same. By the time they are teenagers, and probably a lot sooner than that, they know right from wrong. They know they should be doing their homework. They know they should be taking care of their chores around the house. They know they should be respectful towards their parents. They know they should be kind to, and supportive of, their siblings. It's just sometimes they feel like doing otherwise. This is where helping them develop their ability to discipline themselves can make a huge difference.

Anytime you do something you intended, you exert your will. Any time you do so over the counter thoughts and feelings of your mind and/or body your self-discipline increases. Taking action over protestations such as these is an act of will power. The more you take such actions, the stronger your will gets, and the more self-disciplined you become. Additionally, the more you take these kinds of actions, the faster your mind and your body will learn who really is in charge.

It's sort of little like showing a child who's boss. One of my god-children was seven years old when the family was getting ready to go out to dinner and she didn't want to go. She threw a tantrum, sat herself down, and refused to budge. As the family was leaving the house I picked her up, kicking and screaming, and brought her to the car. As you may have experienced, putting a tantruming seven-year-old into a car seat is not an easy task, and it was not easy for me either. In the midst of her kicking and screaming I got her attention, looked her in the eye, and sternly told her to control herself using "The Voice." She calmed down immediately, at which point, with much validation, I congratulated her on taking control of herself.

This brings up an important point. Earlier when we were discussing discipline and how valuable it is to be very clear with your child about the destination and path you are helping them walk, it is similarly valuable to validate demonstrations of self-control and self-discipline. If you reward such behavior you will increase the chances of them doing it again, as well as help them understand how special, how cool, how valuable self-control and self-discipline are.

Teaching your younger children to show their mind who is actually in control can be a lot of fun. You can turn it into a game. You can find things they don't like to do, then with large quantities of enthusiasm get them to do it, just for the fun of it. When they do it make sure you give them a lot of validation for the self-discipline they showed. If children learn how to do this lightly and easily, they will become more able to do so when their states are not as elevated.

Building Capacity for Self-Discipline

Even if you're on the right track, you'll get run over if you just sit there.

Will Rogers

Being Your Own Boss

As your children get older development of their self-discipline will be more in their hands. There are a number of things they can do to speed this development. As we just mentioned anything they can do to supersede the protests of their mind or body will greatly help. Remember, they are working to develop their **self** discipline. Trying to make them do these things kind of misses the point. Please feel free, though, to encourage and support them as much as they appreciate your efforts.

One thing your daughter could do when her mind is uncooperative is to do much more of the activity than she had intended. For example, let's say she planned to go for a half-an-hour run Saturday morning and heard her mind and body mildly protest, 'I don't feel like it.' If she were interested in developing her self-discipline, she could get herself out of bed and go for a two hour run. If your son intended to read tonight for a an hour and received any blowback from his mind, he could make himself read for three hours. Once their mind gets the message, that if it protests they will do more of what it was protesting against, most of the protesting will quiet down significantly.

Another option that can work particularly well when they have thoughts their mind resists, is to boldly do what they notice their mind is resisting. My hair started to fall out as a teenager. Oh, it didn't really become noticeable until I hit my early twenties. One morning when I was about 25 years old, as I was brushing my teeth and looking in the bathroom mirror I heard a very loud, panicky, thought:

"Oh my God! I'm going bald! I will never get a girl again! Oh my God!"

I did not ask for this thought. I was not intentionally thinking about hair, scalp, or women to the best of my knowledge. I certainly did not have significantly less hair than I had before I went to bed. I just found myself with those thoughts. My response: I shaved my head right then and there. I have kept it shaved ever since.

The result of shaving my head right then was that my mind quieted down for months and the level of cooperation I enjoyed grew exponentially. Taking control in this manner can have great benefits. I would strongly suggest, if you wish to try this out, starting small so your kids can build up their ability to assert their self-control.

Handling Procrastination

Never do something today that you can put off until tomorrow. Are you a procrastinator? How about your son or daughter? I know when I was in high school I put off everything I could until the last minute. Sound familiar? Would you like to be able to teach your children an exercise that will drastically increase their self-discipline and also kill their procrastination?

This is a very simple exercise. It is one of the nastiest, most effective exercises I have ever experienced. It has also proved to be one of the most difficult to perform. The level of discipline it takes can be astounding, especially for a teenager. I have challenged just about every student I have worked with to do this little simple exercise. Only about two out of every hundred students have been successful . . . and their success has reverberated throughout their lives.

So, I put the challenge to you and your children. If either you or they have something that has needed to get done and has been put off again and again, commit to doing this simple two-step exercise, we fondly call:

The Procrastination Killer (Samuels)

Step one: Set a goal to accomplish what it is you have been putting off. (I would suggest picking a relatively small task at first.)

Step two: Shut up. Do not communicate with anybody until you have accomplished your goal.

There it is. The rules of this game require that you do not
talk, text, tweet, e-mail, use American Sign Language, Morse code,
or Navajo code talk until the task is complete. (Of course if the
activity your son has been putting off is talking with his teacher
about a make-up exam, talking with his teacher about the exam
is permitted.) The beauty of this exercise is you never have to
accomplish your goal. No pressure. You just won't be communicating for the rest of your life. Being human, the urge to communicate is immensely motivating, even more so for most teenagers.
Of course, if you or your child actually has monk-like propensities,
doing this exercise may actually have the opposite effect. In my
experience this is rare; almost all of us are powerfully motivated
to communicate.

The 30 Day Practical *(Samuels)*

While the Procrastination Killer develops self-discipline in
short, intense bursts, the 30 Day Practical, (the Practical for short)
develops our ability to discipline ourselves slowly, over long periods of time. The procrastination killer, like a sprint, trains your
children for highly focused, concentrated efforts. The 30 Day Practical, like a marathon, trains them for long-term, sustained efforts
requiring greater endurance. The degree of discipline your children will gain from doing this successfully can be life-changing.

The Practical integrates many of the skills outlined in this
book. Goal setting, planning, attitude control, and the WINS exercise each play a significant role in the 30 Day Practical. And it
certainly takes considerable self-control and self-discipline to be
successful.

The 30 Day Practical involves four groups of activity which
your son or daughter is required to accomplished daily for 30 days
in a row. No breaks are allowed for any reason. They must successfully complete each activity every day. If they forget one, or
for some reason cannot complete one, they begin again the next

day. So, if they have been successful for 18 days in a row and an emergency comes up that precludes them from participating on day 19, no problem. Day one starts tomorrow. Ready? Here we go. One last thing: try it yourself. This is a great exercise to do as a family.

Physical Exercise

The first requirement is to exercise every day. What exercise they do is up to them. They may do the same exercise everyday; they may do different exercises everyday. They may get their exercise by weightlifting at the gym. They may get their exercise doing Pilates at home. They may get their exercise by playing basketball with their friends. It is entirely up to them. The only condition is that what they do is actually exercise for them. So, a walk around the block may be great exercise, if they have never exercised a day in their lives and are just now getting into it. However, if they are a cross country runner, that walk around the block just won't quite do it.

Review Their Goals and Plans

The second requirement is that they review their goals every day. This implies that they have them written down. If they don't yet have goals written down, have them take some time and do it. Make sure that they have goals in a few different areas. Reviewing their goals prepares them for the next activity. Drawing up plans is also a good idea if they haven't done so previously. For the purposes of the Practical, written goals alone will suffice.

WINS

In the chapter on attitudes I introduced the WINS exercise. Here it is to be used as part of the Practical, with only one small change. When it's time to list their 'Next Wins,' for the purposes of this exercise, they need to list 5 tasks they will accomplish during the day that moves them toward their goals. (Younger children can start with 3 tasks.) Here comes the fun part: every day for 30 days in a row they must accomplish those five tasks. If they miss one, once again no problem. Day one starts tomorrow.

If they list more than five tasks, that's fine. They can just select five of those tasks to be the ones that count towards the Practical. As with the exercise portion of the Practical, the tasks they choose have to be meaningful to them and move them towards their goals. Sure, your son could set very simple, extremely easy tasks to accomplish . . .

1. Wake up.
2. Brush my teeth
3. Eat breakfast
4. Watch TV
5. Go to bed

. . . and so cheat himself.

However, if he is going to do this, what's the point? As often is the case in life, a person gets out as much as they put in. For the practical to more fully work its magic, the participant should have goals that are meaningful, goals they are motivated to accomplish.

Having written plans as well as written goals will make the experience that much more rewarding. As your daughter reviews her goals and plans the tasks she needs to set for herself should be fairly clear. It is in this portion of the Practical that participants will readily develop a keen sense for what is possible.

Determining Their Attitude

The final activity is determining the attitude they will approach their day with. This is actually part of the WINS exercise. We separate it out because it is so important. At this stage in the

Practical they simply answer the "S" question from the wins exercise:

"If all this went well what state would you be in." They then do their best to consider this state as they go through their day and review how they did.

The Best Time to Do It

Once they get the hang of it, the Practical should take about fifteen minutes a day or so. Finding the best time to do it every day is critical. Every morning before they leave for school, every evening before bed, or every day after they get home from school and before dinner . . . whatever works. It's up to them. Whatever time they choose, their chances of success will be improved if they can do it at some routine time.

Written Record Keeping

Another requirement is that all participants keep written records. As in the WINS exercise they should have a record for themselves of their performance and accomplishments. It will be great later in their lives for them to look back upon what they were actually able accomplish.

Have your son or daughter pick up something they would like to write in. It could be some cool looking journal; it could be a simple spiral notebook, whatever they feel good about. In the back of their book they should have a list of all their goals and plans so they can access them easily. Why the back of the book? So if they change a goal or write a new plan their updates will still be in the same section as the rest of their goals and plans.

187

Also, make sure each page they use is dated and titled. Each day they should keep a record of:

1. The exercise they did.
2. A confirmation that they reviewed their goals and plans.
3. The WINS Exercise listing all their wins, improvements, and next wins.
4. The attitude with which they wish to approach the day.

Each page might look something like this: (There's something about checking things off that makes us feel good.)

30 Day Practical Day 1 11/20/09

Exercise: Ran 30 minutes √
Goal and Plans reviewed √
W: Completed science project √
   Took out the garbage √
   Read for 1 hour √
   Practiced guitar for 1 hour √
   Spoke with English teacher about my progress √
   Helped friend with math √
I: Been nicer to mom
   Ate a healthier lunch
   Asked Emily out
N: Completed all homework
   Practiced guitar for 1 hour
   Asked Emily out
   Helped mom around the house
   Helped sister with her history project
S: State: Enthusiastic

That's the 30 Day Practical. There is much power to be gained by doing it. Invariably, at some point your son will bite off a little more than he can chew. This is great, for it is at these moments that his discipline is tested. There will come a time, often more than one, where it will be obvious that he cannot complete the tasks he has set for himself this particular day. Now, is the moment of truth. Will he start day one tomorrow? If he does, he passes the test with flying colors. If he does so enthusiastically, he passes the test with flying colors and a bullet. If he takes a few days to lick his wounds and then starts again, he also passes with flying colors. It is with these decisions that self-discipline is built.

There will be other tests. Perhaps it's 10 o'clock in the evening and your daughter realizes she didn't exercise today. She has three choices: she could give up on completing the Practical, she could get out of bed and go work out in the living room, or she could happily start day one tomorrow. Either of the last two receives a passing grade for she will have made a decision that makes her stronger.

A word of caution here. The purpose of the 30 Day Practical is to develop the participant's **self**-discipline. It is on the participant, and the participant alone to complete this. As a parent, you will miss the point if you treat this assignment as if it were homework or a family chore. If your son or daughter are in middle school or beyond, introduce this to them and let them do it on their own. Provide support if they ask, but only if they ask. If your children are younger, they will likely require a little more monitoring and encouragement.

It is best if completing the 30 Day Practical is not made part of a reward structure. If you do so, they will likely end up believing they did this for you. We want them to do it for themselves. It is best if they do it out of their own interest in their self-development. If, however, you wish to reward them for improving their grades and they include completing homework on their 'Next Wins' list, that is all well and good.

If they choose to take this on, pass all the tests that will arise, and complete the Practical they will become very, very different human beings. They will have gained an understanding of their abilities that is as rare as it is exceptional.

.

The Worst/Best Word

In the Teen Lexicon

Obey your parents! Obey your teachers! Obey your elders! We hear that word a lot as we grow up. When we are younger most of us are okay with it. As we get a little older it begins to irk many of us. As we get into our teens a lot of us come to really resist that word.

Of course there are many reasons not to obey those in positions of authority. "Many of those people don't know any more than we do, some know even less," teens have told me. "Often people in authority do not have our best interests at heart," other teens have said. Still other teens have succinctly put it, "They're not my father." Reasonable criticisms all . . . and they all miss the point.

So, why is obedience so important? I have posed this question to hundreds, perhaps thousands of teenagers and young adults. Think about it. Why is it so important to obey? Many students respond by saying obedience keeps us safe, especially when we're young. Others say it's good to obey our seniors because we can learn something from them. Still others say obedience is a sign of respect. All good reasons, though they do not address the most important reason for us to obey.

You see, obedience is a skill. It is a skill that we must develop if we are to be, do, and have what we want. In a few years many of you will be in college, many others of you will be in the workforce. Most of you will be out on your own, which is definitely as it should be. Certainly, most of you are looking forward to it.

Once you are on your own there will be one singular person you will need to obey an order to be successful. That person is you. You will have become your own authority and if you have spent the last six or seven years resisting authority and believing obedience is a bad thing, you cannot but resist your own direction. If you have not developed your skills of obedience you will likely have a difficult time taking orders from yourself.

Why does this matter? Let's say you're in college and the alarm goes off to help get you to class. You don't have to get up; you could skip class. One of the cool things about college is you don't ever have to do anything, you don't have to study, you don't have to take tests, you don't have to write papers, you don't have to do anything you don't want to do. Of course, if you choose not to do any of these activities you will fail.

The same will be true when you enter the workforce. You don't have to do anything you don't want; however if you don't take care of business you will starve. I have known a number of excellent musicians who will practice all day long but don't seem to be able to make themselves hit the streets, knock on doors, and get gigs.

Every successful person has developed the ability to follow their own marching orders. It doesn't particularly matter whether or not they enjoy those orders. In fact, enjoyment rarely enters into it. They all know what needs to get done and they are able to go out and simply do it.

If you are to be numbered among those happy few who have created exceptional lives for themselves, developing the skill of obedience is a must. Once you are actually able to obey simply for its own sake, you can determine for yourself who and what is worthy of your obedience. It is only when you can simply obey for no reason, or for any reason, that you will be truly free to choose.

Epilogue

About 16 years ago I was back east for my brother's graduation. One afternoon we were all hanging out when his six month old daughter started to get fussy. Soon the fussiness escalated and we all took turns trying to calm her down. My sister-in-law took the first crack at it, held her close, gently bounced her on her knee, and lightly tickled her; all to no avail. I took my shot walking around with her and singing Tom Lehrer songs; no change. I handed her off to my brother who proceeded to serenade her with the songs of Allan Sherman; no luck.

It was then that my niece's four-year-old brother came in and told his father to put his sister in the swing. The swing was one of those self-propelled devices that can be found in almost every home where there is an infant. This particular swing seemed to be the bane of my niece's brief existence. Still holding his crying daughter my brother reminded his son that his sister hates the swing but my nephew persisted,

"Put her in the swing, dad."

It was his mother's turn, "Jason, you know she has never liked the swing. She will cry even worse if we try to put her in it."

"Put her in the swing," he said again matter-of-factly.

My brother and sister-in-law looked at each other, shrugged, and put their daughter in the swing. She was asleep in less than two minutes. This was not an isolated event. Again and again in a number of situations Jason had 'known' things. It is to my brother's and sister-in-law's credit that they gave their son the respect to consider his ideas seriously.

When my friend Ron's son was four years old he asked his father, "Dad, did God create us or did we create God?" When he was five he asked his father, "What's more important love or life?"

To which his father responded, "They are both very important. A life without love is not worth living and you can't have love without life."

His son thought about this for a minute looked to his father and said, "You can have love without life. You can love someone who is dead."

Upon hearing this story I suggested to my friend that if the bald men in the orange robes come by his house that he just give his son to them.

Brandon, my engaging seven-year-old friend, is insightful, hilarious, and self-confident in turns. One day he was throwing a ball around with his buddy Cameron during recess at school when his buddy's cousin came by and joined in the fun. Cam had the ball, threw it hard to Brandon, and the ball whizzed by his head.

"Wow!" That was close." Brandon laughed.

"Wouldn't it have been funny if the ball hit me in the nose?"

To which Cam's cousin responded, "Wouldn't it have been funny if the ball killed you."

Instead of letting the boy's comment slide by or worse, starting a fight, or worse still, being hurt by the comment, Brandon went to his friend, told him his cousin's remark was wrong, and that if he wanted to play with him, he would have to leave his cousin. Brandon and his friend went and looked for something else to do, leaving the cousin behind.

My three year old nephew who was tuned into his sister; my friend's five-year-old philosopher son; Brandon who at seven years of age knows when someone is not healthy to be around and can gracefully handle the situation; Brittany who at the age of 12 was concerned about her professionalism; my student Brett who started a business when he was seven years old and at the age of 17 bought his first car with the money he had earned; while these kids are all special to me they are not unique.

Every day tens of thousands, hundreds of thousands, likely millions of children are demonstrating how capable they truly are. Some of them, like the ones above, get to do so growing up in comfortable environments with much support. Others have to do so in harsher circumstances. In single-parent families all across this land 10, 11, and 12-year-old kids are taking care of their four, five, and six-year-old brothers and sisters because their mother or father is working two and three jobs to make ends meet. Teenagers are succeeding at school and working 20 hours a week or more to help their dad or mom pay the bills. These kids are heroic. All of us can achieve great things and rise to almost any occasion if we are asked to, or the situation demands it of us. Our children are no exception.

I maintain an abiding belief that there is nothing children cannot understand, nothing they cannot do. I am committed to engaging even the youngest among them as I would any responsible adult. The only allowance I make is for vocabulary. I truly believe children are quite capable of making agreements and keeping them; I expect even the youngest among them to be responsible and accountable. Much more often than not the children I work with validate my belief in them and live up to these expectations.

Children of all ages are amazing. They can be insightful, generous of spirit, kind, and wise beyond their years. They can also be . . . well . . . kids. With a loving environment, open communication, and the right tools, you can set your daughters and sons on their way to becoming the people that they aspire to be, leading the lives

196

they dream of, and leaving a legacy of which they (and you) will be proud. If you provide all this you can rest easy knowing you have done all you could do to ensure that your sons and daughters enjoy happy, healthy, and fulfilling lives.

My best wishes for you and yours.

Appendix: Selected Exercises

Using Your Imagination (pg 87)

"Are there aspects of my life that are not going well enough for me or that could use some improvement. If so, what are they?"

"What attitude would work best here?"

"What would it be like to operate with this attitude?" or

"What would I be doing differently?"

Recall Exercise (pg 89)

1. "Recall a time you experienced _____ "
   (fill in the state of your choice.)
2. Continue recalling times you experienced that state until your state improves.

WINS (Pg 89)

W: What did you **W**in at yesterday?

I: What **I**mprovements could you make?

N: What will your **N**ext wins be?

S: If all this went well what **S**tate would you be in?

PLANS (pg 116)

P: Purpose and Goal

L: Logic

A: Action Analysis

N: Numbered Steps

S: Schedule

The Four Magic Questions (pg 167)

1. Is there anything I have done that wasn't OK?
2. Is there anything I failed to do that I should have done?
3. Is there anything you did that wasn't OK?
4. Is there anything you failed to do that you should have done?

The Procrastination Killer (pg 183)

Step one: Set a goal to accomplish what it is you have been putting off.

Step two: Shut up. Do not communicate with anybody until you have accomplished your goal.

30 Day Practical (pg 184)

1. Exercise
2. Review your goals and plans
3. Do the WINS Exercise listing all their wins, improvements, and next wins.
4. Decide on the attitude with which you wish to approach your day.

Index

About the Author

Dr. Jay Klusky received his Ph.D. in Cognitive Psychology from UCLA in 1990 under the guidance of Dr. Allen Parducci. Two years later he published his first book, *"Easy A's: Winning the School Game."* In 1974 he began his studies in applied philosophy under the tutelage of Dr. James Samuels, studies which he continues to this day.

Dr. Klusky has lectured at universities, developed and administered alternative high schools for youth considered at-risk, designed programming for those considered talented and gifted, and taught classes for students of all ages. Currently he serves as a mentor/ life-coach/academic adviser, helping parents prepare their children for life after high school and helping teens develop the skills necessary to have extraordinary lives.

If you would like to talk with Dr. Klusky, please feel free to visit his website and set up an appointment. www.jayklusky.com

More offerings from Dr. Klusky:

Personal Consulting:

Could your daughter be more motivated?
Could your son be doing better in school?
Could your daughter be better organized?
Could your son be more focused?

Consult with Dr. Klusky! Dr. Klusky will gladly answer your questions and work with you to resolve any motivational/educational issue you might have with your children. Simply go to www.jayklusky.com and click on the "Consult with Dr. Klusky" button to set up an appointment.

Speaking

Dr. Klusky is a compelling and entertaining speaker. His workshops, seminars, and lectures leave participants better able to prepare their sons, daughters and students for what lies ahead. Have Dr. Klusky to speak to your group. Email him at: jayklusky@comcast.net to make arrangements.

Coming Soon:

On-line videos answering questions that have been posed to Dr. Klusky during the course of his work. These will be short and focused 2 to 3 minute presentations and they will be free.
On-line tele-conferences
On-line radio show

To find out what's new or simply
to get more information go to:
www.jayklusky.com

Also by Dr. Jay Klusky

Easy A's: Winning the School Game

"This is the best book I have ever read on how to study successfully. It's easy to read and apply. The success of my students is testimony to its effectiveness."
Karen Abrams, Founder, Upgrade Academic Coaching

"I've known Dr. Klusky for approximately 30 years, which is all his scholastic life. I always wondered how he did so well in school with so little apparent effort. After reading Easy A's I am pleased that he has been able to set down his methods in a concise, thoroughly readable, and clear blueprint for others to follow."
Gilbert Witte, M.D.

If you found "What Every Parent Wants for Their Child" engaging, you might be interested in "Easy A's: Winning the School Game." It was written for students and speaks directly to them. "Easy A's" is a most accessible and fun read, filled with great tools to help students study, organize, and strategize for college. Like all his work, the focus is on students taking responsibility for their own lives and education.

To order your copy go to:
www.jayklusky.com
or call: 800.937.7771

Made in the USA
Charleston, SC
21 February 2011